The Essence of
CORPORATE STRATEGY

The Essence of
CORPORATE STRATEGY

Cuno Pümpin

Gower

First published in paperback in 1989

Published by
Wildwood House Limited,
Gower Publishing Group,
Gower House,
Croft Road,
Aldershot,
Hants GU11 3HR,
England

Gower Publishing Company,
Old Post Road,
Brookfield,
Vermont 05036,
USA

British Library Cataloguing in Publication Data

Pümpin, Cuno
    The essence of corporate strategy.
    1. Corporate planning.
    I. Title
    658.4′012   HD30.28

Library of Congress Cataloguing in Publication Data

Pümpin, Cuno
    The essence of corporate strategy.
    Bibliography: p.
    Includes index.
    1. Strategic planning   I. Title.

HD30.28.P85   1987   685.4′012   87-14907

ISBN-0-7045-0638-6

Typeset in Great Britain by
Graphic Studios (Southern) Limited, Godalming, Surrey
Printed and bound in Great Britain by
Courier International Ltd, Tiptree, Essex

Contents

Foreword

**by John Ramsay, Director of Strategic
Management Consultancy, Arthur Young**

This book introduces Cuno Pümpin to an English-speaking audience after many years of celebrity among the business communities of West Germany, Switzerland, Austria, Spain and other European countries.

Professor of Business Administration at St Gallen, one of the leading business schools of Europe, Cuno Pümpin has become as well known to companies like Audi, Ciba Geigy and Brown Boveri as the top American corporate strategists, and his personal contribution has been a major factor in their ability to develop and *implement* winning business strategies.

The Pümpin approach is all about successful implementation. It's about concentration on the importance of identifying and cultivating one or two genuinely distinctive capabilities (called Strategic Excellence Positions, or SEPs for short) which can differentiate a company from its competitors and so lead to above average results.

His proposition is that if you really do want above-average performance in the long term, you need first to choose the right SEPs for your particular circumstances and then to imprint them in the behaviour of your organization at all levels and in all functions. Without that level of commitment and participation you too can achieve mediocre results – there's nothing simpler!

We at Arthur Young have enjoyed a very successful working relationship with Cuno Pümpin for many years, during which we have developed a great admiration not just for his vast experience of the practice of strategic management, advising literally scores of major companies, but also for his important contribution to the theory of business strategy and its implementation.

We commend this book to you and think that you will find in it powerful new weapons to carry into the business battlefield of the 1990s and beyond.

Preface

Over the last twenty years the subject of corporate strategy has received a great deal of attention both from managers and from academics. Writers like Igor Ansoff and companies like the Boston Consulting Group developed interesting techniques, and a whole new profession of strategy consulting began to emerge.

Unfortunately, in many cases the strategies based on the new techniques failed to achieve the results expected. The idea of corporate strategy became clouded over by a sense of disappointment bordering on disillusion.

Nevertheless it remains obvious that a sound strategy is a prerequisite for long-term company success. What seems to me to have gone wrong is that consultants and companies were concentrating on strategy development and neglecting strategy implementation.

This impression was considerably strengthened when, in 1982, the now legendary book *In Search of Excellence* appeared. The authors, Thomas J. Peters and R.H. Waterman, showed conclusively that development of superior capabilities is one of the keys to corporate success. It is noticeable that some of the companies they identified in the late 1970s as 'excellent' were running into problems only a few years later. The lesson seems to be that excellence

pays off only if it is acquired in areas that are
strategically important.

Developments like this brought me to the
conclusion that successful corporate management
demands both:

* *Definition of a strategy*, that describes the
  direction the company intends to follow in the
  future. This strategy must state the fields of
  activity in which the company intends to develop
  excellence.

* The *implementation of the strategy*, that must be
  designed such that it really enables the company
  to perform excellently in strategically important
  fields of activity and thus achieve strategic
  superiority.

From these two fundamental principles I
developed the concept of *Strategic Excellence
Positions* (SEPs) and I have put that concept to work
in a management technique which is described in
this book. I believe that SEP management enables
companies to perform better than their competitors
because:

* SEP management is future-oriented.
  Too many companies are managed in a
  defensive way. What our economies need at the
  end of the twentieth century is strategies that aim
  to develop new strengths. SEP management
  produces a positive attitude to the company's
  future.

* SEP management is simple and unbureaucratic.
  Too many companies are managed with
  complex, bureaucratic systems. These systems
  prevent the management from achieving effective
  and creative results. SEP management is easy to
  apply and enables managers to concentrate on the
  key issues.

* SEP management is organic instead of mechanistic.

    Many managers consider the company as a big system that can be constructed and engineered like a machine. Today we know that companies are much too complex to respond to such an approach. We must take an organic view of the company. The main task of the management is to harmonize the different units and use the synergies among them.

* SEP management facilitates strategy.

    The success of a strategy will only be achieved if it is effectively implemented. SEP management focuses on implementation from the beginning.

    For this reason, a considerable part of the book concentrates on ways of involving people in the company and getting results from them. The SEP approach unleashes management energy and helps to convince all employees that together they will lead their company to the top.

    Chapter 1 sets out the principles of corporate strategy derived from a study of both war and business. Chapter 2 introduces and illustrates the SEP concept. In Chapter 3 the ideas of SEP management are presented in the form of ten 'laws of SEP management'. Chapter 4 shows how a company can formulate its own corporate plan based on SEPs and Chapter 5 explains what must be done to ensure effective implementation of that plan.

    It is my hope that the book will help senior executives and corporate planning specialists to embark on a SEP-based programme that will lead their companies to improved performance and increased profitability.

Cuno Pümpin

1 The principles of corporate strategy

Could you imagine Caesar, Wellington or Montgomery at the head of Ford, General Motors or Du Pont? They were certainly chief executives on the battlefield. And if we trace back the principles of strategic management we will find that they all have their origin in the thinking of army commanders as well as great statesmen and scholars. No wonder modern company strategists still compare markets with war zones and first seek to identify their opponents' most dangerous weapons.

The roots of strategic management go back to antiquity. As early as 500 BC the Chinese general, Sun-tzu, put forward a strategic doctrine in the form of instructions called *The Art of War*. The writings of Xenophon on the subject are also well known, and other notable strategists include Caesar, Machiavelli, Clausewitz and Moltke.

It may be useful to recall the principles that need to be taken into account in developing and implementing a strategy.

The similarity of competition on the battlefield and in corporate life is obvious. Suitably adapted, the principles established by writers on warfare are of great value for management. Successful business, like a successful military campaign, depends on:

* determining where and how to attack

* applying the rules of strategy

Let us consider these two aspects in more detail.

Achieving competitive superiority

Competition is a battle for *superiority*. The winner is the better competitor. In a strategic view a company has to decide how to gain the leader position and build up *competitive advantages*. There are two ways of achieving strategic superiority:

* *through differentiation:* occupying a distinctive position in the marketplace.

* *through low costs:* achieving low production costs relative to competitors.

Superiority by differentiation

There are numerous ways of achieving advantage through differentiation:

QUALITY
In its PIMS programme the Strategic Planning Institute examined a large number of company strategies (Schoeffler et al., 1974) and found that firms with above-average product quality tend to achieve above-average profitability (see Figure 1.1).

IMAGE
A company can clearly distinguish itself from its competitors through its product design,

advertising and public relations work. The aim is to build up an image that is superior to those of its competitors so that its product range becomes more attractive in the minds of potential buyers.

DISTRIBUTION

A further possibility is to obtain an advantage over competitors by opening up new distribution channels or developing a better distribution network. Here the aim is to establish a more efficient distribution system and to cover the market better. This can not only lead to higher turnover and cost reduction, it makes the company more attractive to the customer because it is closer to the market.

Fig 1.1 Quality and return on investment. If a company offers products and services of above-average quality (in the customers' view) it will generally be found to achieve above-average profitability (cf. Buzzel, 1978).

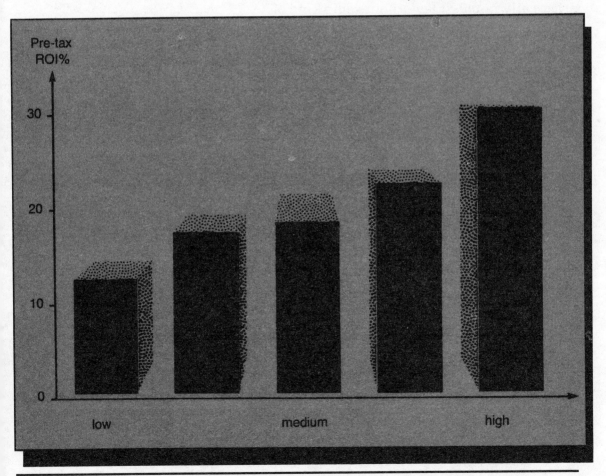

INNOVATION

Innovation is one of the main ways of obtaining a competitive advantage. It enables the company to offer products that are clearly better than those of its rivals. Innovation is therefore a fertile field for the strategic approach. Companies can always expect to benefit from new products that meet customer requirements. However, as a rule, innovation only has a positive effect over the longer term. Over the shorter term it can involve considerable cost.

There are many other ways of achieving differentiation and every company must find its own method for, as Levitt pointed out in his book, *The Marketing Imagination,* successful marketing is practically impossible without some kind of differentiation (Levitt, 1980; Levitt 1983).

Superiority on costs

A company will also achieve a position of competitive advantage if its costs are more favourable than those of its competitors.

IBM, for instance, recognized that costs would be one of the biggest factors in its competitive battle. In the five years up to 1983, the company invested a total of $10 billion in plant and equipment – the equivalent of 5 Nimitz-class nuclear aircraft carriers. That enabled it to move into the position of the most cost-favourable producer (*Fortune,* 13 July 1983).

Strategic research has pinpointed two factors that are of importance here, beyond the straightforward increase in margin. Firstly, the PIMS study (Schoeffler, 1974) shows that, in general, profitability rises with increasing value added per employee (defined as turnover minus costs, divided by number of employees).

Secondly, a 1978 PIMS study (Schoeffler, 1978) showed that profitability also has a strong correlation with investment intensity (defined as fixed assets and working capital, divided by turnover); however, in this case it is an inverse relationship, profitability declining as investment intensity increases. The underlying reasons for this can be traced to the relationship between investment behaviour and cost structure. The manager of a company with a high investment intensity will have less flexibility for strategic action since more of his capital is tied up. He will, therefore, frequently be forced to produce at unfavourable costs, and therefore inefficiently.

These findings from the late 1970s reflect, of course, the relatively inflexible nature of manufacturing investment at that time. It remains to be seen what impact flexible manufacturing systems will have on this relationship.

Relationship between differentiation and cost level

Different combinations of degree of differentiation and level of costs produce different strategic positions. Hall made a study of the US heavy-duty truck industry from this angle (Hall, 1980), (see Figure 1.2).

The study shows that the most successful firms are those with both a favourable cost structure and high differentiation, but that a strategy designed primarily to achieve differentiation, like that pursued by Paccar, can be successful too. Finally, there is the possibility of pursuing a strategy designed purely to reduce costs. Here too positive results can be achieved for a certain time. But firms that neither produce at favourable cost nor achieve great differentiation (White Motor, International Harvester) must expect poor results.

On the basis of the differentiation/cost matrix four different strategic positions can be distinguished.

First, the strategy pursued by companies that can offer quite undifferentiated products at extremely favourable unit costs. For example, Alcan is one of the most cost-efficient aluminium producers thanks to its policy of building smelters in locations with very favourable energy costs. But aluminium is a product that can hardly be differentiated.

Second, the strategy that is designed to achieve high differentiation. Some watch and motor industry firms, such as Rolex and Rolls-Royce, have concentrated on a strategy of comprehensive differentiation. They produce at relatively high unit

Fig 1.2 Differentiation/cost matrix for US truck manufacturers. Companies achieve high profitability with high differentiation and favourable unit costs (from Hall, 1980). ROI in brackets.

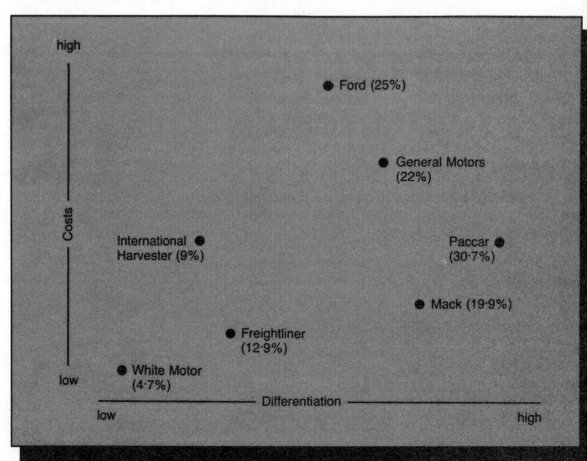

cost but their products are differentiated by their quality and a very strong image.

Third, a company can aim to produce highly differentiated goods with high efficiency. An example is Kodak, which produces photographic materials at very favourable cost but also has a strong trademark image together with high quality, wide distribution and innovation.

Fourth, some firms achieve neither differentiation nor efficiency. Clearly they are crisis-prone, and they make headlines in the press. Notable examples are the European coal and steel industry and the British motor industry in the 1970s.

Each of these strategies has its own financial consequences. Probably the most attractive is a combination of high differentiation with low costs. Next best is a strategy of pure differentiation, the exclusivity of the products enabling the firm to fix its own prices even during the economically difficult times of recession or inflation so as to achieve an adequate return.

Rather less favourable is a strategy of pure cost reduction. Without differentiation, the firm can hardly influence selling prices (unless it is in an absolute monopoly position) and it has to absorb every fluctuation in prices. If, for instance, the spot price for aluminium drops, every aluminium producer will suffer a direct loss of earnings. In 1981/82, the price of aluminium dropped below the unit costs of even the most favourably placed aluminium producers, and even Alcan suffered a loss. It is evident that firms in the lower left of the differentiation/cost matrix are in a very vulnerable position.

The rules of strategy

We have discussed the various types of competitive advantage that a company might seek. Whatever the chosen objective, we need to consider how to achieve it.

Here we can apply some of the rules derived from a study of military strategy. Those that are particularly useful in a business context include:

* Concentrate forces.

* Concentrate on strengths and exploit opportunities for synergy.

* Utilize environmental and market opportunities.

* Match aims with resources.

* Create *unité de doctrine,* motivation, enthusiasm and unity of purpose.

Concentration of forces

The principle of the concentration of forces which Clausewitz established in military strategy has its counterpart in business management, where it can be applied without reservation (Clausewitz, 1980). Why is this principle so important?

* Firstly, only a concentrated use of resources will ensure a *breakthrough* in a particular market. A company usually needs a certain minimum sales volume for a product to be viable – a 'critical mass'. If there are competing products, the breakthrough must be against competitors to achieve a minimum market share. A new product

needs a breakthrough in consumer acceptance, after which catalytic forces, such as word-of-mouth, newspaper articles and so on, play their part in making the product successful.

* Secondly, the concentration of forces is important in the *psychology of learning*. People learn primarily by trial and error. If effort is concentrated on a particular problem then trials will be made and more will be learned about solving the problem.

What guidelines should be followed in applying the principle of the concentration of forces? In military strategy forces are concentrated where the enemy is weak, or where environmental conditions, such as the terrain, are particularly favourable. The same applies to business management. If the objective is a breakthrough in market share then forces need to be concentrated *where competitors are weak*. Japanese car manufacturers in the 1970s, for example, attacked the US firms at their weak point, quality. It would have been pointless to attack one of their strong points such as design.

A company can also concentrate on exploiting favourable factors and especially on meeting customer requirements that are not yet fully satisfied, such as in new technologies, where economic conditions are particularly favourable or where specific customer requirements are not yet fully met. The concentration of forces must be directed at areas where the main competitor has little or no chance of retaliating, or where he has not yet recognized that he is weak. With few exceptions American car makers were hardly aware that they were vulnerable on quality. Another example is the personal computer. At the end of the 1970s the makers of mainframe computers had not recognized the immense potential of the personal computer market. Breakthroughs in that segment of the market were achieved by outsiders like Steve Jobs at Apple Computers. This idea of concentrating on unexpected or unrecognized market segments follows the military strategic principle of the indirect approach put forward by Liddell Hart (Liddell Hart, 1974). Hart studied a large number of major military conflicts from the 5th century BC to the 20th century and established that in virtually every major battle the successful strategy was that of indirect approach, i.e. attacking where the enemy was not expecting to be attacked. The indirect approach has been shown to be a decisive element in the success of many company strategies.

To sum up:

* An essential feature of successful strategies is the *concentration of forces*.

* The forces must be concentrated in areas where *competitors are weak* or where the environmental factors are particularly favourable.

* The principle of the concentration of forces entails an *indirect approach*. The concentration must be such as to enable an *indirect development of forces*.

Concentrating on strengths and exploiting opportunities for synergy

A company's strategy must aim to achieve superiority in specific fields of activity. That superiority is generally reflected in the ability to do certain things better than competitors.

It is clear that a company will be able to achieve this superiority particularly easily where it already has strengths. For that reason available strengths must be carefully assessed to see whether they offer new strategic possibilities.

The principle of concentrating on strengths necessarily entails avoiding weaknesses. A good company strategy is a strategy in which the company's weaknesses (and every company has them) do not matter or play only a minor part.

Related to the principle of concentrating on strengths is the principle of exploiting opportunities for synergy. The word 'synergy' comes from Greek and means 'working together'. The basic idea of synergy is that two or more elements should be combined to create something new, a whole that is more than the sum of its parts, a combination in which $2 + 2 = 5$.

Synergy can be achieved in many ways. One possibility is the acquisition of a company which is active in related fields. However, this involves quite a considerable risk which should not be overlooked. Any combination of activities may produce synergies or destructive conflicts: in some situations $2 + 2 = 3$. Any proposal for combining activities should be carefully examined for possible disadvantages.

In assessing the strengths, weaknesses and synergies of a company, changes in its environment must also be taken into account. A company in the packaging industry had a very strong position in metallic packaging where it was one of the world leaders. But the environmental trend showed clearly that metals were being replaced by plastics. The substitution process left little opportunity for the old material. So what had been the company's strength up to then was rapidly becoming useless. The company was not changing with the environmental and market trend. It had no choice but to concentrate on a weak point, its inadequate knowledge and experience in plastics processing. It had to develop the appropriate capabilities for a new position of strength. Such a strategy is, of course, extremely difficult to implement and it makes very high demands on management, especially in the allocation of resources.

Utilizing environmental and market opportunities

A good strategy must exploit opportunities. That means that before deciding on the strategy a critical examination must be made of the opportunities available in the environment and the market.

In the environment, opportunities may be offered by:

* new technologies

* changing economic conditions

* social trends

* demographic developments

* political changes

* a specific situation in an industry

* customer requirements

* market developments

One of the main concerns of strategic management should be to keep a constant watch for opportunities in the market and the environment and achieve a healthy growth by making proper use of them. The main problem is that, all too often, opportunities are not recognized soon enough. Part of the blame for this lies with traditional or rigid patterns of thought in a company or an industry.

Recognizing opportunities also means *avoiding risks*. Successful strategies are a skilful way of skirting potential threats. A machine tools firm, for instance, was able to avoid the danger of the threat of protectionism by making its machines so technologically advanced that even protectionist countries had to buy from it for competitive reasons.

Matching aims with resources

Military history offers a number of examples of how successful commanders ultimately came to grief because they paid too little attention to matching aims with resources. Perhaps the most famous examples are Napoleon's Russian campaign or Rommel's in Africa.

There are many examples of failure to observe this principle in business life as well. The problem is that many company managements assume that a market system can be stabilized at any point in time. It is not, however, possible to slow down the expansion of a company's activities when financial resources are scarce without causing problems, for every phase of expansion releases its own dynamic, which cannot be stopped at will. Napoleon could not simply break off his campaign in Moscow. In company management, too, there comes a point where there can only be victory or defeat, and here success often depends on whether the critical mass in a particular market, i.e. a certain minimum market share, can be achieved or not. If not, there will be a shake-out in the market as is happening at present in video tapes and personal computers, where many manufacturers with marginal market shares are expected to disappear in the next few years.

Correctly assessing the resources needed to achieve a company's aims is ultimately a question of *estimating risks.* The successful strategist will therefore try to make a careful evaluation of the risks entailed in any particular strategy and where necessary take measures to reduce or compensate them.

Unité de doctrine

Any strategy has to be evolved and implemented by people. Its success will therefore depend on whether it proves possible to motivate the workforce and win their enthusiastic participation so that their efforts are co-ordinated by a unity of purpose.

Even a strategy which may not be optimal in terms of the environment and the market can be implemented with immense success if it has the wholehearted support of everyone in the company – a support that can be a powerful strategic force. An example is provided by the Wal-Mart company. It was able to increase its turnover on the difficult, saturated US retail market from $236 million to $4,667 billion within ten years (1975 to 1984). Its success was probably mainly due to the fact that Sam Walton succeeded in implementing a clear and simple strategy which was admirably suited to motivating and enthusing his workforce. The characteristic feature which is so valuable in this context is most aptly described by the French phrase *unité de doctrine.*

In general, strategies that are simple and homogeneous will produce a strong *unité de doctrine,* while a strategic concept that is built up of a number of divergent business strategies, in accordance with the rules developed for portfolio management, is unlikely to develop a strong *unité de doctrine.*

Summary

The principles of corporate strategy:

1. Achieve competitive advantage through:

* differentiation.

* low costs.

2. Adhere to the basic rules of strategy:

* Concentrate forces

    – on competitors' weak points.

    – on environmental opportunities.

    – through the indirect approach.

* Concentrate on strengths; exploit opportunities
  for synergy; avoid weaknesses.

* Utilize environmental and market
  opportunities, avoiding risks.

* Match aims to resources, estimating risks.

* Create *unité de doctrine,* motivation,
  enthusiasm and unity of purpose.

2 Strategic Excellence Positions

In the 1950s SFS was a small manufacturing company employing about twenty people. At the beginning of the 1960s it decided to use a new fabrication technique and produce special fastenings. The same decision was taken at the same time by a large industrial concern. The technology and the target market were identical for the two firms. Figure 2.1 shows the development of the two companies.

As the diagram shows, the industry giant achieved some initial success. But as a result of the recession in the mid-1970s it abandoned the market. SFS, on the other hand, operating in the same market and with the same technology, was immensely successful. This is reflected not only in a huge increase in turnover but also in a very satisfactory earnings picture. Further analysis of the two companies shows that the industry giant tackled the new project using *bureaucratic* and *technocratic methods*. It did not concentrate its efforts but was content merely to highlight a number of tasks and deal with them routinely. The focus was on the technology which was to generate the turnover.

The result was that the industry giant achieved only very limited recognition of its products in the market. It did not succeed in creating an image as a specialist in the new technique. This lack of a strong image led to unsatisfactory earnings.

SFS, on the other hand, chose a quite different approach. Right from the start it concentrated on identifying *customers' problems* and *developing economic solutions*. For an automotive concern, for instance, it developed a new system of attaching door locks. Although the SFS special screw was more expensive, the simpler attachment technique saved labour time and this lowered the total costs of attaching a door lock by about $0.50 – no small amount in a total production volume of more than 2 million cars with on average three doors each, and a considerable saving for the customer!

This shows that SFS channelled its efforts into providing real *benefit to the customer thereby differentiating itself from competitors.*

Fig 2.1 The development in turnover in the special fastenings divisions of SFS and its main competitor, a large industrial concern.

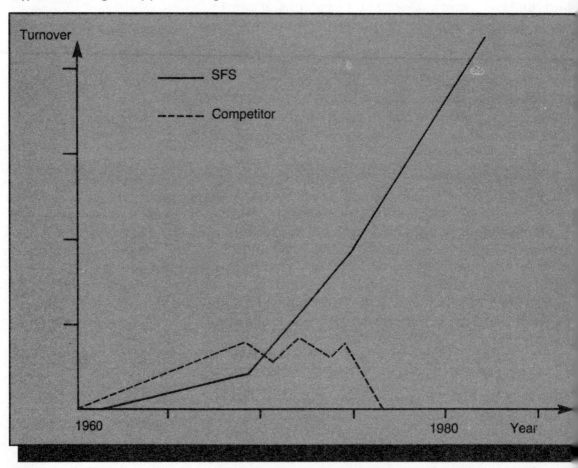

Two conditions had to be met for it to succeed:

1. The SFS management needed to know what factors, from the customers' point of view, would determine market success. It found that it would only have a real chance in the market if it could offer new products that would provide solutions to customers' problems and save costs. The industry giant, on the other hand, contented itself with using the new technique to make the same products it had always made.

2. But the main task was to *develop capabilities* and to achieve excellence so as to establish an image as a firm that could solve customers' problems with an international sales organization that was close to the customer. It was only by working intensively on these elements that the company achieved a market breakthrough.

Strategic Excellence Positions

A company that, like SFS, develops a superior capability in a relevant field of activity achieves a Strategic Excellence Position (SEP). An SEP may be defined as a capability which enables an organization to produce better-than-average results over the longer term compared with its competitors. Corporate strategy must aim to identify and occupy Strategic Excellence Positions, because they are the only basis for superior profitability.

Here, too, there is a close analogy to military strategy. Every general aims to occupy a strategic position and make himself superior to his enemy. In business, positions have to be occupied as well. But instead of territory, the positions are the company's special capabilities.

If you try to achieve excellence in all fields, you spread your forces too thinly and you end up with no excellence at all. Therefore a company must decide on particular points where it intends to achieve excellence. For example, should excellence be achieved in quality or in low-cost production? Each chosen point is a strategic excellence position the company is aiming for. The choice of the field in which excellence has to be achieved is a fundamental strategic decision, perhaps the most important decision a company takes. It defines *the company's direction for the future*. Moreover, it indicates where all the company's forces have to be concentrated. So defining the SEP not only states the goal of the strategy but also shows how to implement it.

Following the basic rules of strategy

The use of Strategic Excellence Positions makes it easier for management to adopt the basic rules of strategy:

* Deciding on a few, clearly defined Strategic Excellence Positions enables a full *concentration of forces*. Resources of material, staff and time can be used in conjunction with, and with direct benefit to, the overall aim.

* The concept of SEP management focuses on a skilful utilization of *existing strengths* and *opportunities for synergy*.

* *Information analysis can be concentrated on utilizing opportunities.* There is little point in trying to reach a Strategic Excellence Position if a competitor has already occupied a leader position there, so SEPs have to be sought where opportunities in the environment and the market are still available and can be utilized.

* Strategic Excellence Positions are built up by the use of resources. *Matching* of aims with resources is an integral part of SEP management.

* Stating the future direction of the company in terms of a limited number of Strategic Excellence Positions gives the staff a clear objective. This necessarily leads to a strong *unité de doctrine,* unity of purpose and motivation.

Where can a company establish an SEP?

A look at the business scene shows that every famous company owes its success to its specific SEP. Successful entrepreneurs focus on strategically relevant factors and with great persistence develop particular capabilities in them. Watson of IBM recognized that service would be crucial and made his company famous for it – with evident success. Rolls-Royce has an SEP in image and quality. Of the large chemical companies Hoffman-La Roche has chosen the psychopharmacology market as SEP while Procter and Gamble's SEP is quality in advertising/communication.

SEPs fall into three different categories:

* *Product-related* Example: A company develops a product, XY, which is superior to those that its competitors produce.

* *Market-related* Example: A company builds up an excellent image in market Z.

* *Functional* Example: A company introduces a new production technology which enables it to produce at favourable cost.

The rest of this chapter examines these three types of SEP in more detail.

It is important to realize that these areas overlap. For instance, by using a sophisticated production technique a company might produce a high-quality product, XY, which enables it to create an excellent image in market Z. The relationship between the three types of SEP is shown in Figure 2.2.

Nor do SEPs need to be restricted to the categories defined here. Often it is the creative and innovative SEP that enables a company to achieve above-average results. There are, for example, many ways of segmenting a market to provide new opportunities.

Sperry Corporation provides a good example of a creative SEP. For years Sperry has been conducting training seminars inside the company and developing other measures under the motto 'The people who listen to you' to make its employees better listeners. The measures inside the company are backed up by a powerful advertising campaign in which Sperry establishes itself as the firm whose representatives listen to the customer and are ready to look into their problems.

Product-related SEPs

THE ABILITY TO RECOGNIZE CUSTOMER REQUIREMENTS

One possible way of developing an SEP is to concentrate on an ability to recognize customer requirements in good time and interpret them correctly.

A company developing an SEP of this kind must concentrate on understanding the market. It must be in a position to recognize new developments better than its competitors. Companies with an SEP of this kind are mainly to be found in industries where customer requirements can

Fig 2.2 The multidimensional view of possible SEPs.

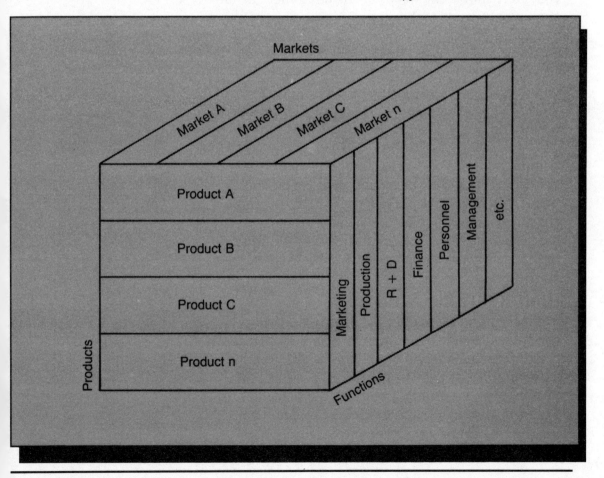

change quickly, something that is particularly noticeable in clothing, where some Italian fashion houses have achieved an unassailable position by developing an SEP of this kind.

THE ABILITY TO PRODUCE GOODS THE CUSTOMER NEEDS

Another possibility is to concentrate on an ability to produce goods the customer needs and develop a Strategic Excellence Position on this. The company should be able to offer a combination of products that the customer regards as optimal. This will generally entail the use of many different raw materials but the central consideration is the needs of the customer rather than a particular technology.

Frühauf is a company with an SEP of this type. It has specialized in lorry bodies. Unlike its rivals, which mainly use aluminium, Frühauf uses a wide range of materials and recently succeeded in producing a new kind of body in plastic.

Segmentation is of central importance in the definition of an SEP based on meeting customer needs. For a company like Frühauf, for example, the question is whether to concentrate on general-purpose lorry bodies or specialize further and perhaps only manufacture bodies for large lorries.

TECHNOLOGY-RELATED SEPs

Following any technological innovation many companies decide to acquire specific capabilities in the new technology and develop an SEP in this. The capabilities may be related to products or processes and a combination is often possible. Firms that concentrate on specific technologies are legion. There are, for example, companies whose entire output is based on the technique of calender rolling. Large areas of the textile industry (spinning and weaving and so on) are dominated by particular manufacturing and processing technologies. Modern industries like semi-conductors can also be clearly identified as based on a particular technology.

MATERIALS-RELATED SEPs

Finally, product-related SEPs can be defined through the materials used. A company can develop its particular abilities in processing certain materials. SEPs of this kind can be found in the plastics industry. For many firms in the aluminium industry as well the main SEP is a commanding knowledge of aluminium metallurgy and processing.

Market-related SEPs

THE MARKET POSITION

Many marketing-oriented firms regard the domination of a particular market as their central SEP. They aim to be the best-established firm in their market and to have the highest market share. A well-known mechanical engineering firm, for instance, aims to achieve a share of at least 40 per cent in every segment in which it operates. Achieving a position as market leader also enables it to be a price leader and so win above-average profit margins.

IMAGE

Recent research has shown that companies that are differentiated from their competitors by a strong image are particularly successful. The firm will exercise a certain gravitational pull and in that sense a positive image can be an important SEP.

There are several examples of firms with image-related SEPs in the consumer goods industries. One of the best known is Dior, which uses its powerful name for a range of products, the common feature of which is the image the name invokes (and its prestige).

Functional SEPs

QUALITY

Quality is the main SEP of many firms that produce high-grade goods. It enables them to achieve a high level of profitability even with a small market share, because the premium paid for the quality is higher than the cost of producing it.

As we shall see later, quality is often more than the result of efforts made by a particular firm; it is also the result of cultural attitudes at national level which set high standards of quality.

SALES

My own empirical studies have shown that about 10 per cent of companies concentrate particularly on building up a highly qualified sales staff and regard this as their SEP. Promoting sales consciousness and an optimal use of the sales personnel are the main concern.

These firms often follow Kotler's sales concept (see Kotler, 1984), according to which products are developed and produced following ideas from staff inside the firm (and not primarily wishes expressed by customers, as is the case with the marketing concept). The sales staff then have to market the products using all their skill at persuasion.

ADVICE TO CUSTOMERS

Firms which build up a consultancy service for customers as an SEP are generally much more concerned with marketing. For them the main focus of interest is not in selling what the firm wants to produce but in providing a genuine benefit to customers through a comprehensive advisory and consultation service. This means that more attention must be paid to customer requirements. A well-known bank deliberately set about building up consultation and advice for customers as an SEP at the time when most of its competitors were not concentrating on contact with customers. As a result it considerably improved its market share.

ADVERTISING

Many consumer goods firms have developed a strong SEP in advertising. Procter & Gamble, for instance, lays great stress on developing and maintaining a highly-qualified staff of product managers who are fully conversant with advertising and its related functions. The firm has developed the appropriate management tools, especially marketing information systems.

DISTRIBUTION

A strong distribution network can constitute a fundamental SEP. In many firms – examples are Avon Products, Caterpillar Tractors and Hilti Fastening Systems – it has been a significant factor in the company's success.

A distribution SEP can be established in various ways. Avon and Hilti each have a direct sales organization dealing with the final consumer. Caterpillar has a worldwide network of contract dealers. Other firms, such as Otto-Versand, have a highly developed physical distribution system.

Walldorf's experience shows that in the capital goods industry particularly a distribution network can be developed as a strong SEP if the company can rely on its own sales organization.

INNOVATION

Innovation is the theme of many SEPs.

One possibility is to create conditions for outstanding achievements in R&D. An SEP can then be based on the introduction of new products. Clearly this is particularly suited to marketing-oriented firms. This SEP was developed strongly by the Swiss chemical industry in the 1950s and 1960s.

Another possibility is process innovation. Developing an SEP in this area may be important for companies making generic products, as in the smelter industry, where the possibilities for product innovation are limited.

A third possibility is to have 'innovation' itself as an SEP. This involves not only a specific type of innovation but innovation on a broad front. All the factors that promote innovation, such as creativity, flexibility and openness to new ideas, must be encouraged as much as possible.

PRODUCTION

The main SEP in the production field is a modern, often automatic production line. This is crucial in the motor industry, for instance. The Japanese automotive firms gained considerable competitive advantages by consistent promotion of production as an SEP. Figure 2.3 illustrates this.

In production particularly, the concern is generally to make optimal use of the experience effect.

SUPPLIES

At a time when raw materials are becoming increasingly scarce, supplies are a matter of growing concern. Skilful exploitation of sources of supply and the development of the appropriate capabilities can constitute an important SEP.

FINANCE

The PIMS study has shown that valuable SEPs can be developed in finance and related areas. Investment intensity has an important influence on the profitability of a firm. If a firm succeeds in achieving an appropriate investment intensity through advantageous financial arrangements it

Fig 2.3 Production of automobiles per employee and year in selected firms (1978).

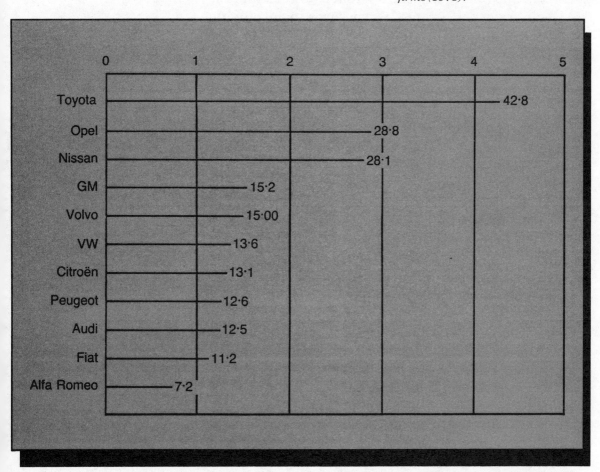

will have an important SEP. Value added also correlates with profitability and a company could establish an SEP by aiming to achieve much more favourable value added than its competitors.

The ability to produce at favourable cost and so achieve cost advantages over competitors is probably one of the most important prerequisites for successful business activity over the longer term. Utilizing every possibility for cost reduction, especially through the consistent use of the experience effect, can be an important SEP.

PERSONNEL

There are considerable differences between one firm and another in the approach to work and the will to work. If a company succeeds in developing these qualities it could have a strong SEP in employee motivation. GM, for instance, achieved enormous increases in productivity and quality within two years in its Buick assembly works, which were notorious for low morale, through a comprehensive work improvement programme.

MANAGEMENT

Finally, management is a potential SEP. A company can concentrate on creating the conditions for long-term business success by introducing appropriate forms of management development. The aim will then be to employ a management staff that is qualified above the average of competitors.

This description of the main categories of SEP by no means exhausts the possibilities. A mail order firm, for example, had an important SEP in a product range that always reflected the latest fashions. A company making specialized technical products succeeded in making very advantageous co-operation agreements with research institutes at various technical universities. The agreements enabled it to profit from work at the frontiers of research in its field. It then had an SEP that was the envy of its competitors.

3 The ten laws of SEP management

The SEP concept provides a basis on which a company's management can plan a profitable future. But how is it applied in practice? This chapter presents my 'Ten Laws for SEP Management', and illustrates them with examples from businesses past and present. The SEP approach will succeed only if these laws are complied with.

LAW 1:
The existence of SEPs determines a company's success.

LAW 2:
SEPs are developed by the allocation of resources.

LAW 3:
The resources allocated to a given SEP must be withdrawn from other possible SEPs, unless there is synergy between them.

LAW 4:
The number of SEPs that can be developed is limited.

LAW 5:
Once an SEP has been developed it can be maintained only if it is constantly nurtured by the allocation of appropriate resources.

LAW 6:
SEPs may stand in a harmonious, neutral or conflicting relation to each other.

LAW 7:
Strong SEPs can only be developed if all the company's specialist managers are involved in interdisciplinary co-operation.

LAW 8:
Developing SEPs is a medium- to long-term activity.

LAW 9:
The benefits of SEPs change over time.

LAW 10:
There is a close relation between a company's corporate culture and its SEPs.

LAW 1:
The existence of SEPs determines a company's success

An SEP may be defined as a consciously developed important and dominant capability of a company which enables above-average results over the longer term in comparison to its competitors.

This first principle shows that a company will only achieve success in the form of above-average results if it has capabilities that can constitute an SEP.

The important word here is *above* average. If several competitors are operating in the same sector and they all have the same positive capabilities they could all achieve good results in a favourable economic climate, but these positive capabilities are not in themselves

SEPs. A company which has an SEP is distinguished from its competitors and superior to them. By virtue of its SEP it will be able to achieve excellent results in a favourable economic climate while its competitors only achieve satisfactory results. Conversely, during a recession, in which the whole sector may be operating at a loss, the firm with the SEP could still achieve satisfactory results.

This was expressly confirmed in a survey I made of 40 leading companies. The results are shown in Figure 3.1.

Fig 3.1 The connection between the existence of SEPs and a company's success – results of an empirical study (Pümpin, 1986).

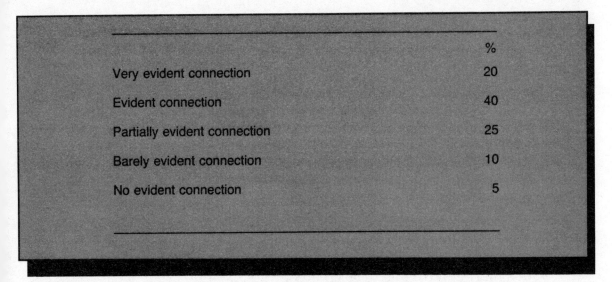

	%
Very evident connection	20
Evident connection	40
Partially evident connection	25
Barely evident connection	10
No evident connection	5

Let us now look at the relation between an SEP and the company's success, using some practical examples.

EXAMPLE 1: TEXAS INSTRUMENTS 1964–78
(see Business Week, 18 September 1978, pp. 67 et seq.)

During the 1960s and 1970s Texas Instruments was one of America's most successful companies. In 1964 its turnover was less than US $400 million. This increased steadily in the following years, reaching $1,000 million in 1973 and a spectacular $2.5 billion in 1978. Profits increased at a similar rate. But in themselves these increases are not exclusive testimony to the company's success. What is decisive is that it is one of the few, out of originally over a hundred, US firms that were able to stand up to Japanese competition during the period in question, and that may in large measure be attributed to its single-minded concentration on two fundamental SEPs: innovation and productivity.

Texas Instruments strengthened its capability for *innovation* with all the means at its disposal and in every aspect of its business activities.

* Its first aim was to acquire absolute predominance in micro-electronic technology.

* Secondly, it promoted product innovation. Its aim was to have the most innovative products in its field.

* Thirdly, it extended innovation to the marketplace itself and developed products for which markets still had to be created.

Specific changes were made to encourage innovation on a broad front. For instance, a salary structure was created which gave particular recognition to innovations and an innovative approach.

With its innovative capability thus secured Texas Instruments was able to offer the market something which surpassed anything its competitors could offer.

The company's second SEP was *productivity*. Competitive conditions were extremely difficult and a firm could only survive if it offered products at prices which compared favourably with those of its competitors. Outstanding productivity was a precondition of success. Texas Instruments achieved this by a skilful combination of unit cost reduction, production technology and investment. Above all, the company proved a master in exploiting the experience effect. It was the only way to gain real advantages, in prices as well, especially over Japanese competitors.

EXAMPLE 2: HILTI AG 1960—80

Today Hilti AG is recognized as the leading manufacturer and marketer of fastening systems for the construction industry. Over the past twenty years it has been able to increase its turnover tenfold while constantly making a healthy profit. Hilti is now the market leader in practically all the fields in which it operates.

How was it able to achieve this success? In addition to a sound business management it concentrated on developing a unique SEP: in the 1950s there was still a widespread retail trade in fastening technology, especially cartridge-loaded machines which fire bolts and nails into concrete and iron. Hilti recognized that, as well as developing machines that were completely safe, it should concentrate on *direct sales,* which would benefit customers because the company could find out exactly what each customer wanted, advise on which product would be best suited and, if necessary, design new products to meet customer requirements.

As a consequence Hilti built up the strongest direct sales organization in the building trade, while its competitors continued to rely on specialist dealers. With its direct sales organization Hilti was able constantly to add new products to its range and so widen the range of services it could offer.

Beside this primary SEP others were also developed, the most important of which were top-quality products and the introduction of modern management methods.

The competitive advantage brought by the SEPs resulted in a steady increase in Hilti's market share. Its strong position enabled the firm to achieve better-than-average results even during the years of recession. Hilti was fully exposed to the exchange rate problems of the 1970s, but their effect was considerably less serious than on other companies which had weaker SEPs.

IMPLICATIONS

Law 1 states that there is a connection between an SEP and a company's success, and this has been illustrated with examples. The law has some important implications for management:

1. The first task is to define the target. Are the average business results normally obtained in a particular sector enough or should the company be aiming for above-average results in the longer term?

   If average results are enough there is no need to develop SEPs. The management is content to stay abreast of its competitors. If above-average results are required there is only one course: develop a strong SEP.

2. Law 1 also shows the importance of the SEP concept in general. The aim of business studies should be to show how to achieve above-average results. The strong correlation between SEPs and corporate success means that the SEP will necessarily become an important management technique. Stressing the importance of an SEP in management must not, however, allow familiar and proven business methods to be neglected. The main purpose of the SEP is to show where the focal points lie and where effort is to be concentrated.

LAW 2:
SEPs are developed by the allocation of resources

Resources are the means available to management to fulfil its function. In this context resources such as personnel, plant and finance are of predominant importance but in addition to these classical resources, as they might be called, there is management time, which is possibly the most important resource of all.

It is a feature of all business activity that it produces from third parties through the input of resources. However, an input of resources alone is not sufficient to guarantee success. If the company is to be successful, the resources have to be allocated in the way that produces SEPs.

The relation between the allocation of resources and the development of SEPs can also be seen clearly in the theory of the experience curve (Henderson, 1974), according to which the unit costs of production drop by between 20 and 30 per cent each time the cumulative quantity of production is doubled. A high cumulative production volume in comparison with competitors will therefore enable cost-related SEPs to be developed. But Henderson expressly states that experience effects will only occur if management does everything in its power to reduce costs. In other words resources in the form of financial investment, personnel (e.g. training) and especially management time must be concentrated on exploiting the experience effect to develop an SEP.

The same principle can be applied elsewhere and it will be possible to achieve experience effects – or, better still, *SEP effects* – in relation to other criteria such as product development, sales organization, customer advisory service and so on, by cumulative work on the problems involved. The firm that allocates above-average resources to the criterion in question and makes best use of its SEP will acquire the strongest competitive position.

EXAMPLE 3: ZELLWEGER AG 1960–80

Zellweger is a leading manufacturer of specialist electronic products. It has a strong position in all its main markets. Its central SEP is its ability to produce top-quality high-technology equipment, and this was developed over many years of intensive work. The firm allocated its resources as follows:

* *Production* Plant and equipment were improved to secure this SEP. For example, NC machine tools were acquired and used to give flexibility in the production of the company's specialized products. The firm deliberately built up a stock of machinery that was versatile and could be used flexibly in the service of its SEP.

---

* *Quality* Working groups were set up to increase the reliability and quality of the products and make evaluations and deal with the problems. A group would consist, for example, of the development engineer, a designer, a member of the work study department and the foreman.

* *Personnel* Great weight was attached to training. Internal seminars were held which were expressly designed to develop the capabilities needed for the SEP. The importance of the SEP was stressed repeatedly in all training programmes.

* *Management* However, the central focus of the allocation of resources was management time. The managing director concerned himself personally with the efforts being made to develop the SEP at all levels. He also made sure that the other management staff concentrated on what was needed for the SEP. The progress that was being made was regularly monitored in 'Product Conferences' which the managing director attended. A feature of the conferences was that virtually all levels of management were represented. This was the only way of achieving the necessary depth.

EXAMPLE 4: UNIKELLER AG 1955–80

Unikeller AG is the leading European manufacturer of sound-insulating material for the motor industry. Over the past twenty-five years its turnover has risen from a few million dollars to more than $150 million. Results of this magnitude could not be achieved without first-class technical know-how in the field of noise reduction. Unikeller therefore concentrated its resources on developing 'know-how' as its SEP.

The company recognized that if it was to keep up with the tremendous developments in the motor industry in the 1950s and 1960s it had to devote time to:

*   direct contact with the development departments of car manufacture.

*   training in the unfamiliar area of automobile acoustics.

*   converting the knowledge acquired into products and services to be fed into the market.

*   ensuring a supply of new developments in products and services for the phenomenal increase in automobile production.

With the automobile industry being accorded such priority in all the firm's policies, targets and programmes the appropriate financial resources had to be provided for research, development and application technology, and here no expense was spared. The company has successfully withstood two recessions in the automotive industry since 1973, an indication of how wise it was to choose that path.

IMPLICATIONS

Law 2 states that SEPs can only be developed by the allocation of resources and it has the following important implications:

The SEP is so important for the future of the company that all its available resources must be allocated with this target in mind.

Whenever resources are allocated, it should be asked whether the way they are being allocated will really contribute to developing the SEP the company needs. In other words, the SEPs must *serve as criteria in any decision* on the allocation of resources.

This means that resources cannot be allocated purely on financial grounds, which would suggest, for example, that in investment decisions only the question of profitability or pay-back time should be considered. It must be borne in mind that an allocation of resources solely on financial grounds entails a great danger of fragmentation, since it would be possible to allocate resources on financial grounds to serve several different SEPs. Considering individual investment projects in isolation may lead to a decision that is not optimal for the company as a whole.

The rule that resource allocation must be taken into account does not apply only to decisions that will have a long-term effect and are of great importance. Management must also think in terms of SEPs when taking decisions with a short- or medium-term effect and importance, for these apparently insignificant matters often add up to a considerable involvement of funds. Moreover, 'minor' decisions of this nature often develop their own dynamic and take up resources to an extent that was not anticipated.

To what extent is this observed in practice? My own survey (Figure 3.2) revealed that most of the companies questioned (63 per cent) do in fact base their most important decisions on their corporate strategy (and so presumably take account of their

SEPs) but far fewer firms (34 per cent) take their overall strategy into account in medium-term decisions and only 5 per cent base decisions of minor importance on their corporate strategy.

To sum up: Law 2 leads to the conclusion that:

* Allocation of resources must take account of the

Fig 3.2 Reliance on the corporate strategy in taking decisions of various types (as a percentage of all companies questioned).

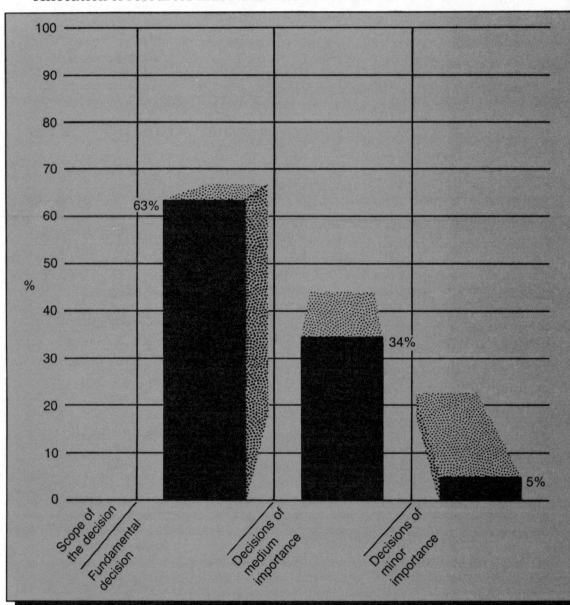

SEP and not be decided by criteria of profitability alone.

* Managers must be aware that resources are being allocated even in short- and medium-range decisions. These too, therefore, must take account of the SEP.

LAW 3:
The resources allocated to a given SEP must be withdrawn from other possible SEPs, unless there is synergy between them

This law can be illustrated by an example. Let us assume that a management would like to develop simultaneously 'quality' and 'favourable production costs' as SEPs. The first requires quality controls, staff training and so on, while the second can only be built up with cost-favourable production methods, raw and auxiliary materials obtained at favourable cost and so on. Different activities are therefore needed to build up the first and second SEPs.

Remember that any particular resource is available once and once only. That applies to funds (each individual pound or dollar), equipment (each single machine) and personnel (each hour of an employee's time). The principle is particularly evident in the prime asset of management time; Peter Drucker has pointed out that the supply of management time is totally inelastic: each minute of management time is available only once and not again.

For our example it follows that a member of the team cannot be employed on pursuing 'quality' and 'favourable production costs' as SEPs at one and the same time. Nor can the same pound or dollar be spent on both targets at once. So if time and funds are being spent on 'quality' they must necessarily be withdrawn from the other potential SEP, 'favourable production costs'.

In general it can therefore be said that any unit of a resource that is allocated to one SEP will have to be withdrawn from other potential SEPs and is no longer available for them.

There is an important exception to this in the form of *synergy*. If there is synergy between two SEPs the pursuit of one of them can have a positive effect on the other. If, for instance, I would like to develop both 'quality' and 'customer advisory service' as SEPs, the external consultancy staff I shall have to build up will have a positive effect on both the quality of the advice and the productivity of the advisory service. Close attention must therefore be paid to the synergy between SEPs. It will now be clear that SEPs relate to each other in different ways (see Figure 3.3).

EXAMPLE 5: THE FORD MOTOR COMPANY 1906–27

Between 1906 and 1924 Henry Ford pursued a policy of cost reduction with the utmost consistency. In other words, Ford developed 'favourable production costs' as an SEP.

To that end he first had to dismiss some top managers who favoured a high-price policy. Then he began to design his famous Model T. His greatest achievement was to develop new, cost-cutting production methods (the conveyor belt). But he also took advantage of the other possibilities for cost reduction such as a high utilization of capacity, optimal purchases and

---

the use of appropriate plant. Concentrating entirely on cost reduction enabled Ford to drop his real prices by more than sixfold between 1907 and 1926. Direct working hours per vehicle dropped from 65 in 1913 to 31 in 1922 and between 1910 and 1921 his market share rose from 10.7 per cent to 55.4 per cent! The

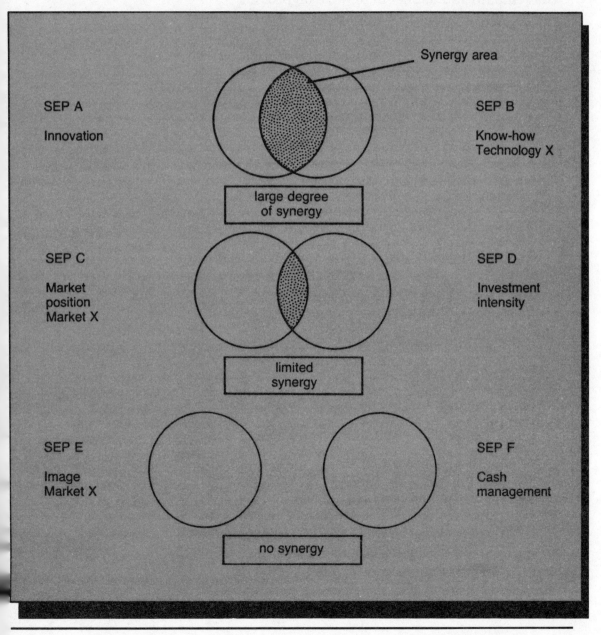

Fig 3.3 Synergy between SEPs.

huge success brought by so single-minded a concentration on cost reduction was bound to entail a withdrawal of resources from other possible Strategic Excellence Positions, and this is very evident in innovation. Between 1910 and 1925 Ford was not in a position to present a significant product innovation. On the contrary, the company did not begin to work on product innovation again until its competitors (GM and Chrysler) had already taken the lead. The consequence was an enormous drop in Ford's market share from 1923 to 1927, from 55.4 per cent in 1921 to 10.6 per cent in 1927 (Abernathy and Wayne, 1974).

EXAMPLE 6: INVESTA LTD 1949–80
(for reasons of confidentiality the company's name has been changed)

Investa Ltd was founded in 1949. After beginning with general fitting work it started to concentrate in 1954 on the production of components used in the construction industry and was able to develop and patent an important new product. This product gave it virtually a monopoly position in the market between 1955 and 1967. The increases in turnover and profits were far above the average for the industry.

During the 1960s the owner of the firm had the idea of producing the measuring equipment needed to test his components himself and he then began offering these products on the international market to third parties. Again the company was very successful, and between 1970 and 1980 it was able to build up its position in the world market for this measuring equipment from zero to 50 per cent, with a massive rise in turnover. But it was only possible to develop this new SEP by withdrawing resources from the construction components. The board meetings, for example, were almost exclusively concerned with the measuring equipment and most investment expenditure was in the new product area. The result was that the company began to lose its market shares for construction components as from 1970 and by 1980 its market position had shrunk to less than 30 per cent. It was only possible to develop the new SEP 'measuring equipment' by withdrawing resources from the SEP 'construction components'.

IMPLICATIONS
Law 3 has three important implications:

1. Any allocation of resources, whether they be financial, material, personnel or – and especially – management time, must be considered in relation to the company's SEP. The main question is therefore: Does this resource allocation help the company develop its SEP? The question is of crucial importance, for resources once allocated are no longer available for other SEPs which may be more important.

2. The SEPs that are to be developed must be chosen with the utmost care; moreover, they must be clear to all the management, so that they can allocate their resources appropriately.

3. Synergy is of fundamental importance. The disadvantage of having to withdraw resources can be mitigated and actually turned to an advantage by taking all the opportunities for exploiting synergy.

LAW 4:
The number of SEPs that can be developed is limited

In principle it would be desirable for a company to have as many SEPs as possible and so be superior to its competitors over a wide field, but simple logic shows that this is only possible in very exceptional cases.

It follows from the definition of the SEP that it must always be seen in relation to competitors. A firm's competitors will certainly use their resources for activities that are of particular importance in the given environment. Therefore, a company that spreads its resources over a wide area will be in an inferior position to one that concentrates its resources. It is, then, an inherent law of the free market economy that success can be achieved only by a concentrated use of resources, taking into account the given environment and market situation. It follows that it is not possible to develop an unlimited number of SEPs.

The need to concentrate forces on a few Strategic Excellence Positions has been formulated in various ways in management literature. Peter Drucker in particular has pointed this out: 'Every creator of a large enterprise known to us, from the Medici and the founders of the Bank of England to Thomas Watson of IBM in our own time, had a clearly defined idea . . . of the company, and this determined his actions and decisions' (Drucker, 1974). The 'idea' is no more than the central SEP of the firm which the owner wanted to develop. It should be noted that Drucker only mentions one idea, and this, too, is an indication that the number of SEPs that can be developed is extremely limited.

In a very much more recent empirical study, Thomas Peters (Peters, 1980) has reached a similar conclusion. He points out that particularly successful firms are characterized by the fact that they concentrate their activities in one field. He cites the examples of the former president of the Dana-Corporation, Rene McPherson, whose main concern was productivity, and Patrick Haggerty of Texas Instruments, who pushed primarily for 'innovation' as an SEP.

Of course these firms allocate resources to other fields of activity as well, but their special feature is that each company's top management gives priority to one SEP above all others and concerns itself intensively with the work involved. In that sense it is correct to speak of a concentration of resources on one strategic excellence position. The others are subordinated to and derived from the central position.

EXAMPLE 7: THE HEAD SKI COMPANY 1950–70

In the 1950s and early 1960s the Head Ski Company was the most successful manufacturer of ski products. It was able to increase its market share from 1 per cent (1950) to over 20 per cent (1964). Besides the major innovation of metal skis at the end of the 1940s this success was largely due to two SEPs:

* great emphasis on the quality of the skis, and

* the creation of a strong sales organization through specialized dealers.

Other SEPs, such as further innovation, advertising, cost reduction, modern production methods and so on, were deliberately pushed

---

into the background. In the mid-1960s Head embarked on a number of acquisitions. What is interesting is that the company was in no position to make a success of this diversification. It simply did not have the necessary capabilities. When it then began to try to develop (as an SEP) there was not enough strength left to maintain the former SEPs. As a result the company's market share in the ski sector dropped to less than 10 per cent and the decline went so far that Howard Head ultimately had to sell his company.

EXAMPLE 8: THE CATERPILLAR TRACTOR CO. 1950—80

Caterpillar is one of the world's largest producers of earth-moving, construction and materials transportation machinery and is generally regarded as one of the most successful US companies. In fifty-five years of activity (till 1980) the firm only once made a loss and that was during the slump in 1932.

An analysis of the history of the firm shows that its primary SEP is its worldwide network of accredited dealers. This has ensured a customer service that is unique in the industry. Spare parts can be supplied to any customer anywhere in the world within 48 hours. In the investment-intensive capital goods sector this is a crucial factor. Another SEP is its top-grade, reliable products and the company has worked intensively to develop this as well.

Concentrating on the service network and product quality necessarily meant that other fields of activity had to be neglected. Labour relations were a cause for concern for years and despite intensive efforts the company was not able to build these up as an SEP. Labour relations remained a weak point and in 1979 came a protracted and bitter strike, with 40,000 workers withdrawing their labour for 11 weeks, greatly to the detriment of the company's earnings position.

The emphasis which the firm put on developing two major SEPs meant that Caterpillar was not in a position to build up others. The need to improve labour relations was evident for years but no progress was made.

IMPLICATIONS

The fourth law is also of crucial importance for management. It implies that management must decide what is to be their company's SEP. If this is not done, there is a risk that the company's resources will be divided between too many potential SEPs and no real strength can be developed.

The recognition that many of the most successful firms develop and maintain one absolutely central SEP suggests that it would be advisable to grade SEPs in different categories. One SEP must be at the centre of management's approach and this can be called the 'primary SEP'. It needs to be supported by others and they can be called 'secondary SEPs'. This is illustrated in Figure 3.4.

LAW 5:
Once an SEP has been developed it can be maintained only if it is constantly nurtured by the allocation of appropriate resources

Having developed an SEP for itself a company must expect its competitors to strike back. This is very evident in the motor industry, where the Japanese manufacturers in the 1960s and 1970s had 'quality' as an SEP and used it to gain an advantage over American firms. At present, new SEPs, such as styling and technology, are the focus of attention and the American and European manufacturers will only be able to maintain their positions if they can keep the advantage they have gained. They are currently discovering how difficult it is.

Companies develop SEPs in a continually changing world and must adjust their strategies as the world about them alters. A company that tries to freeze a position once gained will suddenly find itself catapulted to the rear. This can only be prevented by constant attention to the SEPs that have been developed and

Fig 3.4 Supporting the primary SEP with secondary SEPs.

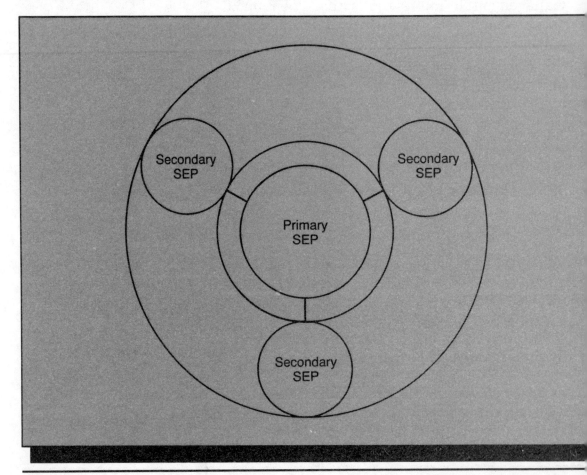

consistent efforts to develop them further (see Figure 3.5).

Law 5 is an application of one of the basic rules of strategy – the one that says you must concentrate on strengths. It means not only that in general it is pointless trying to convert weaknesses into strengths but also that strength, once developed as an SEP, needs constant care and attention and *must be developed further*.

Fig 3.5 The dynamic of an SEP. If a company fails to develop its SEP further at time t_1 (straight line) it may be presumed that Competitor X will catch up at time t_2. The SEP will then lose its usefulness. An SEP must therefore constantly be developed (broken line).

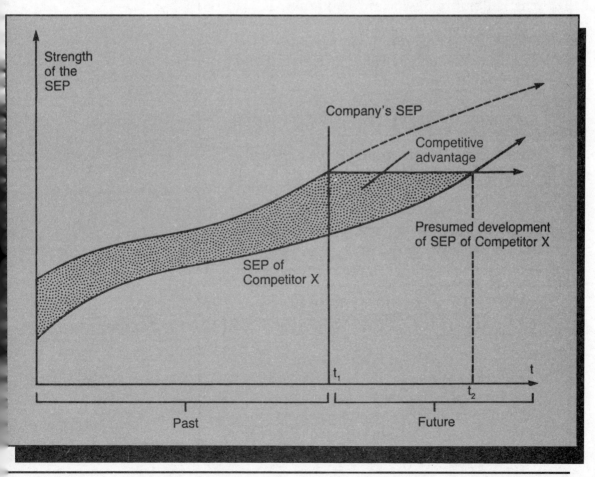

EXAMPLE 9: SWISSAIR 1955—70

In a paper presented to the St Gallen Graduate School of Business Administration the former Chairman of Swissair, Dr W. Berchtold, explained the efforts he had made to develop and maintain the high standard of quality in service which was a principal SEP of his airline. His remarks made it plain that it was only possible to maintain a leading position in quality with constant care and attention and intensive efforts to develop the quality further. Some of the measures used were:

* permanent training for all the staff, in which particular stress was laid on quality.

* constant emphasis on the importance of top-class service in memoranda to the staff and other publications.

* systematic control of the standard of quality.

* stress on quality in innumerable personal contacts between Dr Berchtold and his staff.

Only constant emphasis on quality enabled Swissair to develop and maintain its reputation as one of the very best airlines.

EXAMPLE 10: PRECISION INSTRUMENT CO. 1960—78
(company's name changed)

Precision Instrument is an old-established international company. In the 1950s and 1960s it was directed by B. Owen, who had an excellent reputation as an ambitious and far-sighted manager. Until his term in office came to an end in 1972 he insisted that great weight should be laid on top quality and professional selling. The firm was regarded as the market leader in these fields and thanks to its efforts was able to build up a strong market share, with profits and growth rates well above the national average.

In 1972 Owen retired. Shortly afterwards the company was taken over by a conglomerate. The new management wanted even greater profitability and growth and embarked on a number of measures including opening new markets, revising the production programme, opening new sales channels and more stringent cost control. Naturally they were concerned to maintain the existing high level of quality and service. But the shift in emphasis meant that the existing SEP was not given the same attention as before. A survey in 1978 showed that two competitors had caught up with or surpassed the firm in quality and selling. Precision Instrument had lost its lead in these two areas. It had been able to achieve a slight increase in profitability and growth but competitors had been able to take away considerable market shares in its traditional products.

IMPLICATIONS

It is often assumed in practice that once an SEP has been developed it can be taken for granted, and it is then concluded that other SEPs can be developed as well to maximize profits, but as this discussion of Law 5 has shown, an SEP is dynamic. SEPs must always be seen in comparison to the position of competitors and as a rule any neglect of an SEP will enable competitors to catch up. Advantages gained are then lost.

Even more dangerous is a situation where corporate thinking and action slacken when positive results are obtained after intensive efforts to develop an SEP and the management think they can rest on their laurels. Then the company may not even attempt to develop new or further SEPs and it is only a matter of time before more aggressive competitors have caught up. This can be seen in countless examples of once-successful firms.

As we shall see, an SEP that has once been developed should only be neglected if changes in the environment or market conditions show that it is not likely to be of any further use. If an SEP does become obsolete following changes in requirements, new SEPs have to be developed. In that case the management will naturally take the decision not to concentrate any more on developing a particular SEP. In fact, steps often have to be taken to dismantle an obsolete SEP.

Law 6:
SEPs may stand in a harmonious, neutral or conflicting relation to each other

We saw when discussing Law 4 that it is possible to develop primary and secondary SEPs and that a company should restrict itself to as small a number of SEPs as possible. In practice it is, however, often necessary to supplement a primary SEP with secondary SEPs. What effect does this have on the choice?

As soon as more than one SEP is required – even if only two or three – they must be chosen to one consistent system. SEPs are never developed in isolation but in the context of day-to-day management practice. Employees, customers and other interested parties will always be testing the actions of the management to see if they are inherently consistent. The top management must bear this in mind when deciding what are to be the company's central SEPs. These SEPs can stand in different relations to each other:

* In the ideal case the SEPs that are to be developed will be in a harmonious relation to each other and in that case work spent on developing SEP A will benefit SEP B. That would happen if the primary SEP is innovative capability and the secondary SEP is a high market share in a new market X. There will be harmony because new markets generally can be successfully opened if the products to be sold are of an innovative nature, or if the market is opened with innovative measures. In that case there is clearly synergy between the two SEPs.

* A second possibility is that the two SEPs stand in a neutral relation to each other. In that case developing SEP A will not be of any particular benefit to SEP B, though it will not hinder it in any way either. An example of this is if 'sales organization' is to be developed as an SEP as well as 'production technology'. Each can be developed independently of the other.

* Finally, the SEPs that are to be developed may be in a conflicting relation to each other and work on developing SEP A may interfere with efforts to achieve SEP B. An example of this is a case where 'marketing image' is to be developed as SEP A with 'advantageous costs' as SEP B. Since a marketing image can generally only be achieved with considerable expenditure on advertising and public relations these efforts will be directly contrary to efforts to cut costs. It is obvious

that conflicts and contradictions can arise in such situations.

A company's management must recognize these three basic possibilities. Only then will it be in a position to lay down appropriate guidelines for the selection of its own SEPs.

EXAMPLE 11: PLASTIC CO. 1950—81
(company's name changed)

Plastic Co. was established in the 1920s. It engages mainly in the mass production of plastic goods for a wide range of customers and at present employs about 500 people. During the 1950s and 1960s the main emphasis was on the most rational production methods, and an excellent accounting system was introduced which enabled the management to embark on a comprehensive programme to cut costs. It was then able to pursue the appropriate low-price policy. The internationalization of markets in the 1970s meant that Plastic Co. had increasingly to compete against large foreign firms which were able to offer goods at even lower prices because of the quantities they produced. Plastic Co.'s profitability suffered as a consequence.

In the face of this situation the company changed its policy in 1973 and stress was laid on two factors:

* First, it was recognized that the pressure of international competition could only be met by increased innovation. A working group for new products was formed which embarked on an active search for new possibilities and initiated a number of projects.

---

* Secondly, the company decided to intensify its traditional policy of lowering costs. Every possibility of reducing costs was utilized with the help of consultants.

The results were inevitable: the new product projects were blocked on cost grounds before they could have any effect. In 1981 the situation was as follows:

* Not a single new product had been introduced over the past five years.

* It had been possible to lower costs slightly. But it had not proved possible to counter international price pressure in any way and the earnings situation was still unsatisfactory.

Plastic Co. had been trying to develop two conflicting SEPs, exhaustive utilization of cost reduction as well as innovation. This meant that all its efforts at innovation were bound to fail and that the aim of minimal costs could not be fully achieved because considerable expenditure was incurred in the abortive attempts at innovation.

EXAMPLE 12: JAKOB FUGGER, THE RICH 1479—92

In 1479 Jakob Fugger joined the famous firm of merchants founded by his father. The firm already had a strong SEP as the best sales organization in Europe. The Fuggers had agents in all the main trading cities.

The discovery of gunpowder and the cannon were enormous innovations at the time and they opened up completely new markets. Jakob

Fugger immediately recognized the immense importance that copper would have in the next few decades as a raw material in cannon manufacture and he decided to go into mining. At first sight this was a completely different business. But Jakob Fugger proved brilliantly capable of harmonizing the new SEP 'mining' with the old SEP 'sales organization', and he was able to gain considerable competitive advantages by selling the ores through his sales organization. The advantages were so great that he was able to build up a monopoly in copper in Europe. He created the conditions that enabled his firm to achieve a turnover equal to 10 per cent (!) of the gross domestic product of Germany at the time (Ogger, 1979).

IMPLICATIONS

Law 6 shows that a primary SEP must be chosen in such a way that secondary and even tertiary SEPs can be added as harmonious extensions to it. Only in this way can the desired synergy be achieved.

If a management does not keep to this rule and attempts to develop conflicting SEPs it will run the risk of its efforts cancelling each other out with unsatisfactory results. In that case it has not utilized any potential there may be for synergy. But the synergy potentials are often of immense importance in acquiring real competitive advantages.

There is also an important strategic principle in favour of harmonizing envisaged SEPs. One characteristic of successful strategies is that they lead to a 'unité de doctrine' within the company. Conflicting SEPs are not consistent with each other; this can lead to confusion among the employees and lack of unité de doctrine.

Law 7:
Strong SEPs can only be developed if all the company's specialist managers are involved in interdisciplinary co-operation

Business and management studies are still strongly functional in orientation, and universities and management training institutions tend to offer largely functional courses such as marketing, production, finance, personnel and so on. This means that the functional element tends to predominate in the practice of management as well.

As a consequence, top managers tend to adopt specific approaches, according to where they were educated, and in many cases their thinking is highly compartmentalized.

However, this tendency to specialization is evident in other respects as well and similarly one-sided attitudes can be observed in sectors that have established their own particular training, such as banking and insurance.

Such a one-sided approach can hamper the development of SEPs:

* First, because an orientation to a particular management specialism means that the importance of SEPs which go beyond that specialism is often not recognized – this phenomenon can be called *corporate blindness*.

* Secondly, too one-sided or compartmentalized an approach on the part of the management hinders the development of the SEP. This is of particular importance if we remember that SEPs should not be determined by the criteria of a particular management specialism or

company unit but by environmental and market conditions.

From what has already been said it will be apparent that every area of a company's activities must make a contribution to developing its SEP. Figure 3.6 shows the relationships involved. For example, if a company producing consumer goods is developing 'image' as its central SEP all the functional areas of the company must play their part.

The same, of course, applies to product-related SEPs. Here too all departments must make their contribution. In this connection

Fig 3.6 The contribution of the different management functions to developing an SEP.

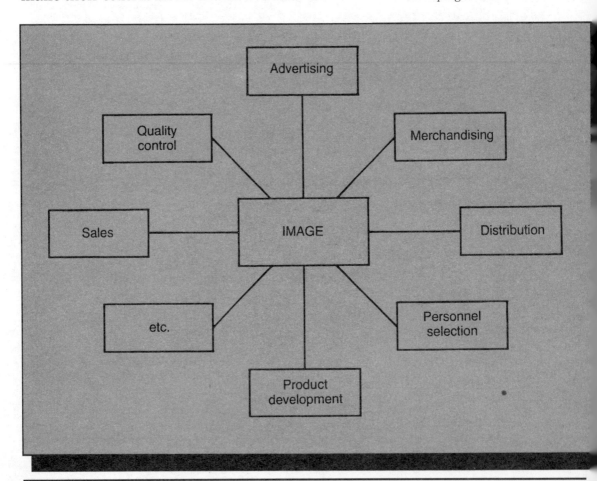

attention must be paid to the definition of the SEP. If, for example, a company is concentrating on developing the product-related SEP 'lawn-mowers' then, according to Law 7, all the functional areas must make a contribution and the co-operation must be across divisions and subject areas.

As Figure 3.7 shows, attention here focuses on an SEP which does not correspond to any one functional unit of the company. All the areas of the company's activities are used to develop this SEP, and the aim is to develop, produce and sell a product that is superior to anything that competitors have to offer.

Fig 3.7 The interdisciplinary development of the SEP 'lawn-mowers'.

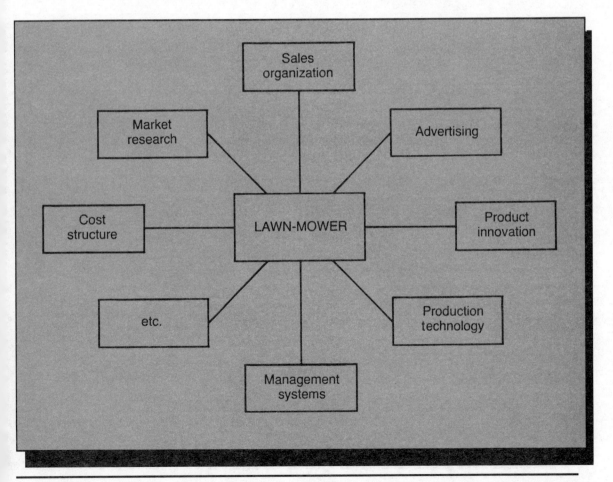

'Lawn-mower' is a technologically-based concept. Adopting it as an SEP could mean that technical features or considerations are always in the foreground, resulting in a one-sided orientation to technology, which will in turn hinder an interdisciplinary approach. From that point of view it might be better to use a market-related definition. Figure 3.8 makes this clear. Here 'lawn care' has become the central consideration and now the lawn-mower is only one element among several. A wealth of different disciplines can contribute to the development of this new SEP.

It is already clear that thinking in terms of SEPs will help to overcome the arbitrary

Fig 3.8 The interdisciplinary development of the SEP 'lawn care'.

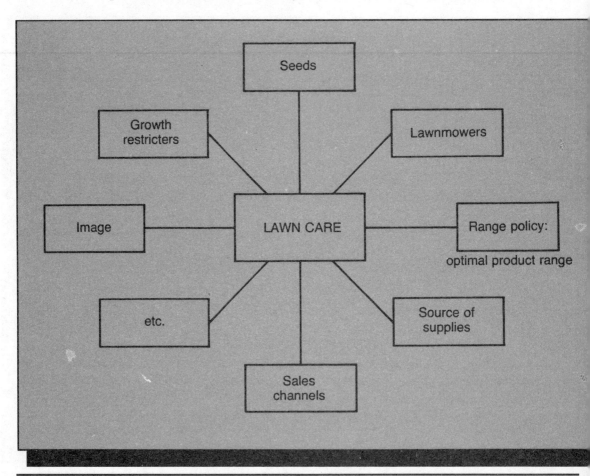

functionalization of the training system in
many companies.

Why is a more interdisciplinary approach so
essential? A company always has to face
problems in its market and environment which
do not in any way correspond with the internal
structure of the company, such as its division
into functional areas. Market and
environmental changes result from
physiological, psycho-sociological, economic
technological factors. The simple fact that, as a
rule, several of these factors will arise in
combination in any given case demonstrates the
need for an interdisciplinary approach. It is only
possible to find comprehensive solutions if a
wide range of disciplines are involved.

EXAMPLE 13: TQC – TOTAL QUALITY CONTROL

The huge success of Japanese manufacturers
is very largely due to their leading position in
quality. In 1951 Edward Deming gave a number
of lectures on the subject of quality control as
part of the American reconstruction programme
(Deming, 1981). The principles he outlined were
adopted by Japanese managements and
developed during the 1960s and 1970s into the
concept of *total quality control* (TQC). The main
feature is that quality control is no longer
regarded as the task of one functional unit: it is
an integral activity. Hirosuke Hiraoka,
Executive Vice-President of Komatsu, said: 'For
us total quality control extends from the first
market survey to after-sales service. We want to
satisfy our customers and keep our costs low'
(Gray, 1981). Total quality control is therefore
no less than total interdisciplinary co-operation
between all the functional areas of the company
in the service of quality. In practice many

Japanese companies, in entertainment electronics, for instance, and photography, have succeeded in building up strong SEPs in the quality field with interdisciplinary TQC.

EXAMPLE 14: AT & T 1905—15

At the beginning of the twentieth century one of the most successful businessmen in American industry, Theodore N. Vail, said of the American Telephone and Telegraph Company (also known as the Bell system): 'Our business is service.' This comment in fact defined the company's central SEP, and characterized a comprehensive, interdisciplinary approach to the problems the company faced. Research, technology, finance policy, staff training and public relations were all directed to the same end. It was only this interdisciplinary approach to the goal of service that enabled AT & T to achieve its main target and prevent nationalization. Had the company not been in a position to offer its customers a genuinely satisfactory service the USA would presumably have gone the way of every other country and nationalized the telephone service like the postal service. Recognizing the right SEP and consistent work in developing it were the central prerequisites which enabled the company to survive (Drucker, 1974).

IMPLICATIONS

Law 7 has two important implications:

1. It is clear that excessive specialization is not advisable. Only the manager who takes a general view will be in a position to recognize the main areas where an interdisciplinary approach is needed in the work of developing an

SEP. Specialists who are delegated to interdisciplinary working groups must also increasingly adopt a broad approach. That is the only way to evolve meaningful solutions in co-ordination with their colleagues.

2. A bias to particular specialisms or occupations on the part of the top management can be extremely dangerous. It may ultimately mean that the work of developing SEPs is too one-sided. It is known that a one-sided approach by top management is one of the main causes of company failures (Argenti, 1976).

These considerations will obviously have an important part to play in management selection and training, where more attention must be paid to a broad spectrum of knowledge and interests. A highly productive step which will have a directly synergetic effect is to make the SEP the company wants the central theme of internal training and handle it in an interdisciplinary way.

Law 8:
Developing SEPs is a medium- to long-term activity

Medium term means a period of three to five years; long term is a period of five to fifteen years or even longer.

Law 8 states that an SEP can only be developed with consistent efforts that extend far beyond the short term. Only in rare cases will it be possible to develop an SEP in two to three years; on the contrary, it must be expected that periods of five, ten and even more years are necessary to create the prerequisites for a successful business.

The reasons for Law 8 can be found in the definition of an SEP itself, according to which an SEP is a capability of a company which allows it to achieve above-average results. This means that a capability can only be regarded as an SEP for as long as firms producing comparable products or working in comparable market segments do not have the same capability. As soon as a competitor develops the same capability, by definition it can no longer be an SEP.

Obviously, a company would gain very little from developing an SEP in an area in which one or more of its competitors could follow within a very short time. A characteristic of strong SEPs is that it will take several years before competitors present any threat to the company. But normally a position of this nature can only be achieved after years of intensely hard work. In my own survey of 40 companies the average time required to generate an SEP was 5.3 years. Figure 3.9 shows the average times for specific fields of activity. It should be noted that these figures are averages. My enquiry covered periods of up to 15 years.

EXAMPLE 15: AVON PRODUCTS 1960–80

Avon Products is now the world's largest producer and marketer of cosmetics. It acquired its leading position thanks to an excellent system of direct selling. But the decisive breakthrough did not come until the 1960s after decades of work building up the direct sales system.

In 1980, Avon had more than 1.25 million women sales representatives who 'bring quality, value, fashion and service to millions of customers in 31 countries throughout the world'

(Annual Report for 1980). It is noteworthy that Avon was always aware of its SEP. In 1971, for instance, new products in the form of costume jewellery and accessories were included in the range because they were products that could be sold to the existing customers through the direct sales network. The expansion was a complete success.

EXAMPLE 16: BMW 1945–63

In the 1950s BMW was still producing motorcycles and luxury cars with the image of a traditional and somewhat old-fashioned

Fig 3.9 The time needed to develop an SEP (Pümpin, 1986).

Time needed to develop particular capabilities	
in production	4·3 years
in marketing	4·4 years
in internal organization	4·6 years
in innovation	6·6 years
in service	4·8 years
in distribution	5·0 years
in management potential	7·0 years
Average	5·3 years

manufacturer. A market analysis showed that it would only be able to survive if it re-oriented. A new company strategy was therefore drawn up, the main element in which was the development of an SEP in the form of a new image. BMW wanted to project itself as a manufacturer of high-quality performance cars. The necessary decision was taken in the mid-1950s and it took no less than eight years before its new image was recognized and accepted by the market (Ball, 1980).

IMPLICATIONS

The development of an SEP normally takes a long time, and the decision to develop an SEP involves certain considerations:

* Firstly, it is extremely important for the management to recognize that the success of a company depends on the existence of an SEP. Only if this is clearly recognized will it be possible to generate the effort and energy needed to develop the necessary capabilities in the company and sustain them over an extended period of time.

* Secondly, it is evident that choosing the SEP to go for is a very big decision, because generally at least five years will pass before it bears fruit. If the decision was the right one then above-average results may be expected. If it was wrong then the time that has passed between taking the decision and the end of the re-orientation work must be regarded as time irrevocably lost. Firms that have to recognize they have not succeeded in building up a strategic excellence position, or that it is inadequate or the wrong one, must come to the painful conclusion that they have been set back by several years. In this connection it must be remembered that the choice of SEP to develop is

a matter for the top management. Since a managing director is rarely in the job for longer than ten to fifteen years he is hardly likely to be able to take more than two or three of these basic decisions in the time given to him. One wrong decision is therefore of dramatic importance, not only for the company but even more for those at the top who have to take the responsibility, for they will seldom have time to make any real corrections.

* Thirdly, it follows from the long period needed to develop an SEP that the work must be pursued resolutely and steadily. If all the resources available are used to this end considerable savings in time can be achieved. In certain competitive situations this can be of crucial importance.

Seen as a whole, Law 8 is a clear warning to managements not to concentrate on short-term success. In sectors where short-term considerations tend to predominate, companies which adopt a strategic approach should have the advantage.

Law 9:
The benefits of SEPs change over time

Law 1 showed that the success of a company is largely determined by the SEP it has developed. Whether or not an SEP is successful depends on whether it is the right one for the company's environmental and market conditions. If there is complete accord, the benefit (in the form of cash flow, growth in turnover and improvement of the market position) will be correspondingly large.

Environmental and market conditions are continually changing. There is thus a great danger that SEPs, once they have been developed, will, after a certain time, no longer correspond to changed conditions. This in itself shows that a company must check constantly whether its SEP still accords with the market and the environment or whether there is a risk that it is becoming obsolete. It also means that new SEPs that are envisaged must correspond to the medium- and long-term developments that may be expected in the market and the environment.

A particular problem in this regard is that in recent times market and environmental conditions have been subject to turbulent change (see e.g. Ansoff, 1979). There is, therefore, a growing danger that an SEP may be obsolete before it has been completely developed. Is there then any point in aiming to develop SEPs at all? Yes there is, for three reasons:

1. The environment and the market will always need specific services. The SEP concept of management is therefore directed to developing in the company specific capabilities to provide these services.

   Unlike long-term planning, in which the extrapolation of quantitative trends is emphasized, the basis of SEP management is to align the company to the development of particular capabilities. It is in fact much easier to make a qualitative forecast of capabilities that may be important in the future than a quantitative prediction.

2. A period of turbulent change in the environment forces a company to concentrate on capabilities that are absolutely essential and their development.

3. An SEP is deliberately described in very broad terms. The SEP 'image', for instance, includes the company's capability to build up an effective image. If environmental conditions change the company should therefore be in a position to build up a strong image, perhaps for a new group of products, fairly quickly.

EXAMPLE 17: GENERAL MOTORS 1920–27

In discussing Law 3 we made a brief acquaintance with the US automobile market. We saw that between 1906 and 1921 Ford concentrated all his resources on developing 'capability to manufacture low-cost automobiles' as an SEP. The policy won him a 55.4 per cent market share in 1921. In 1920, by contrast, General Motors had a market share of 17 per cent and this had dropped to 12 per cent by 1921 (Abernathy and Wayne, 1974). In this dramatic situation, which was accompanied by heavy losses, the management decided to develop a new product concept and introduce it to the market. The decision was taken on 9 June 1921 by the Management Committee, and its core element was to develop a product range consisting of six brands of automobiles, each with a specific price range.

In 1923 fundamental changes occurred in the American automobile market. Over the preceding twenty years customers had in the main wanted a basic means of transport at as favourable a price as possible. By the beginning of the 1920s so many cars had been sold that a considerable second-hand market had grown up. Customers who only wanted a basic means of transport could find what they wanted in this market at a low price, while the considerable

---

rise in purchasing power over the same period meant that customers who wanted to buy a new car were looking for an individual vehicle.

In this situation General Motors' decision to embark on a new product policy moved it into a much more favourable strategic position than that of Ford, whose Model T continued to be geared largely to the demand for a basic mode of transport. While General Motors had created an SEP which was ideal for the market in the first half of the 1920s, Ford discovered that the SEP it had developed between 1910 and 1920 no longer corresponded to the new market conditions. As a result Ford's market share fell from 55 per cent in 1921 to 10.6 per cent in 1927, while General Motors' share grew from 12 per cent to over 40 per cent (Chrysler was also very successful during this period) (Sloan, 1964).

EXAMPLE 18: DE SEDE 1965–78

Furniture manufacture is one of the oldest sectors of Swiss industry. It consists of about 200 producers, most of whom are members of furniture manufacturers' associations. The main feature of the industry during the 1950s was that individual firms made a full range of products (living-room and bedroom furniture). Only a few firms specialized. Most of the manufacturers produced for the retail trade and their main aim was good quality at favourable cost. Very few pursued an image or marketing policy since the furniture was sold through local dealers.

But in the 1960s the market changed because of a considerable rise in purchasing power which was reflected very largely in greater individualism and a more personal approach to home design. Suddenly the demand was for the individual lifestyle. Lüthi, a small furniture manufacturer, recognized this in 1964 and concentrated all its efforts on creating a strong brand image as its central SEP. The measures it used included:

* concentration on lounge suites

* concentration on a particular material (leather)

* developing design

* promoting the 'de Sede' trademark in the market.

This strategy enabled the firm to make full use of the changes in the market and the turnover of the de Sede group rose from around $1 million in 1964 to over $40 million in 1979. De Sede became the world market leader for lounge suites and achieved a profit rate far above the average by utilizing experience effects.

Most of the Swiss furniture manufacturers who did not adjust their SEPs to the new circumstances lost their position and massive market share.

IMPLICATIONS

Law 9 has a number of implications for SEP management:

1. Companies that have already developed SEPs – and my own researches show that most companies have done this even though they

may not use that terminology – must ask themselves very critically whether these SEPs will still be beneficial in future.

2. If new SEPs are to be developed they must be geared comprehensively to the environmental and market conditions that are to be expected in five, ten or fifteen years' time.

3. In a turbulent environment repeated short-term changes are only to be expected and in such cases two possibilities are open to the firm:

   * It can consciously build up flexibility as an SEP, allocating all its resources to achieve maximum flexibility.

   * It can ignore short-term fluctuations and concentrate unswervingly and consistently on the SEPs which should be best suited to environment and market conditions over the longer term.

   It would certainly be wrong to change direction like a weather-vane at every change in the climate. A policy of this nature would mean that no SEP would emerge at all.

4. Environmental and market developments must be under constant review to identify those that are relevant for the SEP. If this reveals opportunities for new SEPs or a threat to existing ones the appropriate decisions must be taken. An adequate early warning system should be created to enable the changes to be recognized in time.

5. In the current climate it is to be expected that the environment will change in unforeseen ways. This means that different capabilities will frequently be demanded of the firm and for that reason it must be ready to adjust to developments of this kind.

LAW 10:
There is a close relation between a company's corporate culture and its SEPs

The corporate culture is all the values, opinions and norms in a company which determine the behaviour of its employees (Deal and Kennedy, 1982). They are 'unwritten laws' and obedience to them is demanded – consciously or unconsciously – of the employees, while failure to observe them results in sanctions or some other form of disadvantage.

Corporate culture norms relate, for instance, to how certain tasks are to be undertaken in the organization. One leading multinational company, for example, requires extremely detailed quantitative planning for any investment project. In a somewhat smaller but very dynamic company, however, detailed information on such matters as quality improvement, the innovation advantage to be hoped for and so on is required.

A corporate culture also includes norms on the appearance and demeanour of employees inside and outside the firm. It often regulates questions of dress and other apparently minor matters. In one well-known marketing company it is these 'minor' factors which decide questions of promotion and financial advancement for employees who come into contact with customers.

Generally a corporate culture will tell us what kind of behaviour is regarded as very important in a particular firm and which is of less significance. Several authors have pointed out that this can vary greatly from one firm to another.

What is the significance of the corporate culture for the SEP?

* Firstly, the corporate culture is a comprehensive, psychological phenomenon. It comprises a variety of informal rules and attitudes. Primarily, it is a framework of norms and values that are held by employees, have evolved over time and are often unconscious.

* The SEP, on the other hand, relates to the company's potential for certain capabilities which already exist or are to be created and which are directed to achieve clear advantages over competitors in the market. An SEP is therefore a strategic asset, while the corporate culture is a psychological phenomenon in the organization.

Why is there a close interrelation between the SEP and the corporate culture? The main purpose of the SEP is to achieve above-average capabilities in a specific field in comparison to competitors. This is only possible if the signals given by the management are all consistent and add up to a coherent whole. In other words, the system of norms and values which make up the corporate culture must correspond to the SEP that is desired. The interrelation is such that an SEP can only be developed if there is a corresponding system of values inside the organization. Equally, the development of an SEP will have a clear impact on the corporate culture.

There are two further aspects to be considered:

* Firstly, companies that have undertaken a strategic re-orientation which did not

correspond to their corporate strategy have had the greatest difficulty in implementing the strategy. General Motors was one company that discovered this. As early as the 1960s a team under John De Lorean advocated pushing ahead with small automobiles. Although the emphasis was right and this helped General Motors to defend its market share in the 1970s, the enterprise failed because the corporate culture was centred around full-size cars (De Lorean, 1980). In another case, a qualified general manager was summarily dismissed because he expounded a strategy which did not accord with the corporate culture the president had spent decades building up.

* A second problem arises with companies with a cost-oriented corporate culture. They are often so geared to short-term ends that they have no time for strategic thinking (or to build up an SEP) and here it can be shown that the corporate culture may actually prevent the management from thinking and acting in accordance with a strategy.

EXAMPLE 19: AT & T 1975—81

The story of AT & T from 1900 to 1920 has been used to illustrate Law 7. More recent developments illustrate Law 10.

The main aim of Theodore N. Vail was to build up service as a central SEP. The strategy created a deeply rooted corporate culture which still had an effect by the end of the 1970s. It can be seen in the way service problems are tackled and solved with the greatest sensitivity and speed. Probably no other private (and certainly no public) telephone company reacts so quickly

---

to a customer's desire to have a telephone installed. This extreme emphasis on service was also evident when the telephone exchange in Manhattan broke down. AT & T immediately sent in 4,000 workmen, and 3,000 tons of equipment were delivered within a very short time. Normal telephone service was resumed within 22 days.

Performance of this calibre is only possible if all the capabilities of the company – in addition to the pure allocation of resources – have become a corporate culture.

But this also involved problems, as was evident from the developments at AT & T. By order of the Federal Communications Commission other firms were then permitted to sell products which competed with AT & T for its communications network. This was a new kind of competition for AT & T, since these firms were offering not only a service but also individual solutions to customers' requirements. But AT & T was a company that had sold virtually only mass-produced products. It was difficult for the management to change the corporate culture and develop a marketing approach in which more attention would be given to individual customers' requirements.

This example shows that the relationship between corporate culture and business strategy is crucial. Great attention therefore needs to be paid to the corporate culture in the management of an SEP.

EXAMPLE 20: GENERAL ELECTRIC 1970–81

Under the leadership of its chairmen, and in particular its last chairman, Reginald H. Jones, General Electric has over the last thirty years developed a finance-oriented culture. Every effort has been channelled into building up the company's financial strength as an SEP. To that end General Electric's famous financial planning system was introduced, together with strict financial controls and other finance-oriented measures. The results were extremely positive from a financial point of view; despite two recessions profits trebled over ten years, with ROI on average 50 per cent above that of competitors.

But the extreme dedication to the SEP 'financial strength' and the creation of a corresponding corporate culture brought setbacks in other areas. In the consumer goods division the market share for dishwashers, for example, fell from 26 per cent in 1974 to 18 per cent in 1980. The quality of the product also suffered from the severity of the financial controls. On his retirement on 1 April 1980 Jones admitted that the corporate culture needed to regain the lead it had lost in high technology markets and for that reason John F. Welch, an engineer biased towards technology and innovation, was elected as the new chairman. His task was to redirect the culture that had grown up from the concentration on finance and build up a strong SEP in 'technological and innovation capabilities' (*Business Week,* 16 March 1981).

IMPLICATIONS

As we have seen, there is a very close relation between the corporate culture and a company's SEPs. Great attention must therefore be paid to the corporate culture in strategic management. Firstly, this means analysing the existing culture to identify its nature and orientation. Once the new SEPs that are to be developed have been decided on, a critical review is needed to ensure that they correspond to the corporate culture. There are several possibilities:

* There may be complete accord between the corporate culture and the new SEPs. That is the ideal situation. Let us suppose, for example, that a company with a sales-oriented culture decides to strengthen direct sales. In this case work can start immediately and intensively on building up the SEP.

* There is a neutral relationship between the corporate culture and the new SEP. This will be the case if a company with a distribution-oriented culture decides to construct the SEP 'innovation capability'. Distribution and innovation are not inherently contradictory nor will they obstruct each other. Nevertheless, in such a case it will be necessary to develop an innovation-based culture gradually.

* The corporate culture and the new SEP are incompatible. That will be the case if a company with a pronounced costs and finance culture wishes to construct an SEP which relates to innovation. This is probably the most difficult situation and here the management must ask whether it will be possible to establish the SEP at all. In some cases the obstacles will be so great that the efforts are not likely to succeed; in that case it would be advisable to construct as an interim measure an SEP that is in a neutral

relation to the corporate culture. But if the management does decide to go ahead with an incompatible SEP it will need to devote considerable attention to how to implement it. Comprehensive training measures will probably be needed and some key posts will need to be refilled.

Law 6 implied that there must be a harmonious relation between SEPs that are to be developed simultaneously. As Law 10 shows, that in itself is not sufficient. Care must also be taken to ensure that the SEP that is to be developed relates harmoniously to the corporate culture.

The ten Laws outlined here provide the basis for the whole process of strategic management. The next chapter considers how to choose which strategy to follow.

4 Building a strategy

This chapter shows how to decide the appropriate SEPs for a company. Developing SEPs is a medium- to long-term activity (Law 8) on which the company's success depends (Law 1). So selecting what to develop as an SEP and formulating a description of it are important matters requiring the attention of the whole management team. The basic rules of strategy emphasize the importance of knowing all about the company – its strengths, capabilities and weaknesses – and the environment – the opportunities it offers and the ways in which it is likely to change. The process of determining SEPs for a company naturally starts with gathering and analysing information about the company and its environment. This is such an important phase of the planning process that the first half of this chapter is devoted to it. The information gathering and analysis provide the basis for applying the principles of corporate strategy in the formulation of a grand strategy for the company, and that is the subject of the second half of this chapter.

The technique of acquiring information

What kinds of problem arise in strategic management? Clearly it is concerned first and foremost with recognizing important *developments and trends.* This entails looking at the situation as a whole, adopting a qualitative view. The ultimate aim of business, however, is to make a profit, and profit is quantitative. It is calculated from turnover and costs. Each of these has numerous component elements that have to be measured separately before the total can be calculated. It is necessary to ask what the potential turnover in a particular market segment is and what cost structures will be entailed in each business activity.

What is needed for strategic planning, therefore, is an information analysis that will identify general relationships and interconnections in the environment, in the economic sector or industry and in the company's requirements, but which will also facilitate the quantitative surveys that are needed for market forecasts and company budgeting.

Information can be obtained in a variety of ways, including desk research, personal interviews, surveys/questionnaires and using consultants. It is dangerous to rely on just one technique, and the best results are probably achieved from a mixture of methods.

Information can be obtained both from inside the company and externally. Many useful data can be taken from trade periodicals, specialist literature and so on. Similarly, data already available inside the firm can be analysed. Other, qualitative, aspects may be covered in conversations with selected managers and employees.

In some cases this very simple method will suffice but it should be borne in mind that psychological factors can distort the analysis. Unwelcome information can be suppressed and positive factors overplayed. Established patterns of thought can also lead to a situation being misinterpreted.

Many firms always tackle strategic problems in the same way. They also try to solve new problems with their established patterns of thought and that is why new developments are often first recognized by outsiders, who exploit them to their own profit, while the older firms are stuck in traditional modes of thought and unable to do so. Let us take one example: In 1837 the Surveyor of the Royal Navy, Sir William Symonds, expressed the following view of the screw propeller: '. . . even if the propeller had the power of propelling the vessel, it would be found altogether useless in practice, because the power being applied in the stern it would be absolutely impossible to make the vessel steer' (see *The Futurist,* December 1968). Sir William held to his view, although screw-propelled vessels had already successfully been put into operation at the beginning of the 1820s and it was evident that the new system worked. Many experts were not prepared to accept this evidence, and as a result a number of British shipyards continued to concentrate on improvements to sailing ships. It was an engineer from outside the Navy, Isambard Kingdom Brunel, who designed the first large steel screw-propelled steamer. As a result of the new technical development many traditional shipyards found themselves in financial difficulties.

Similar events can be found in other industries. The first electronic clock, for instance, was developed by the Swiss clock-making industry, but the management of many of the old-established firms simply could not imagine that it would prove to be a great breakthrough and they did not market it. As a result the Swiss clock industry lost a massive share of the world market and firms in Japan and Hong Kong took over the lead.

So we must keep asking ourselves whether and to what extent unexpected breaks in the trend are to be expected. The management of a company must be aware that its patterns of thought are built up over many decades and that as a consequence it may fail to recognize new developments. For that reason *external generalists* should always be consulted when a strategy is to be developed, for they will not be imprisoned in the patterns of thought traditional in any particular industry.

It is also advisable to supplement the subjective assessments with objective, scientific methods. Questionnaires will, for instance, give a much more precise picture of the corporate culture than conversations and personal opinions. The same applies to cost studies and market analyses, where quantitative surveys can be very valuable.

To create a good information analysis it is important to use all available sources and techniques. This often requires ingenuity and skill. That is very much the case in the analysis of competitors, where it often seems at first that the information required can be obtained only by industrial espionage. However, this may not be necessary: a creative approach can often yield highly interesting information about competitors in a perfectly legal way.

Naturally every information analysis must cover a strategically relevant period of time. Developing a strategic excellence position is a medium- to long-term process, and the information analysis needs to take into account developments and trends in the environment and in the market over a period of three to fifteen years.

Content of information analysis

The purpose of gathering and analysing information is to provide a basis for the application of the principles of corporate strategy. From this point of view, both general and specific information are required: general to indicate trends and structures, specific to give precise data on costs, numbers of potential customers, etc.

Figure 4.1 shows the kinds of information needed.

The process of gathering and using information for strategic planning involves the following steps:

1. an analysis of the company itself, its capabilities, strengths, costs, strategies pursued in the past and corporate culture.

2. an analysis of the environment: the general environment, the industry in which the company operates, its market and its competition.

3. an analysis of the needs and expectations of the stakeholders.

4. an analysis of this basic information in terms of the company's strategic objectives to identify the success factors in the market, possible new activities for the company and key strategic problems.

5. from this, a definition of the SEP and overall strategy.

The following paragraphs discuss each of these steps in detail.

Company analysis

CAPABILITY ANALYSIS

The strategic success of a company depends on its Strategic Excellence Position and the capabilities this represents (Law 1 of SEP management). For this reason the first step is to analyse the

Fig 4.1 Information analysis for strategic planning.

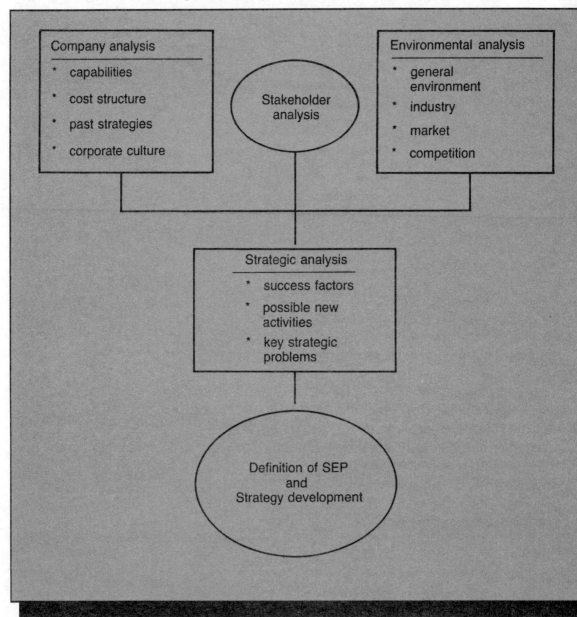

company's capabilities to show in what fields of activity the company's own capabilities may be superior and in what areas other firms have already occupied Strategic Excellence Positions. The capability analysis should also give information on what opportunities there are for synergy which could be exploited by the new strategy. Finally it should reveal to what extent the company has funds and resources of its own available for the strategy. The capability analysis should cover both the present state and the past development of the company.

Once again it is very important to be aware of possible psychological barriers in a company which can mean that conditions inside the company are always perceived and assessed with traditional or established patterns of thought. This means that there may well be discrepancies between subjective opinion inside the firm and reality. In an effective capability analysis, therefore, precise figures are needed to substantiate subjective opinions, and a capability analysis must always take the form of a comparison with competitors. Figure 4.2 is a checklist of possible items to include in the capability analysis.

COST STRUCTURE ANALYSIS

Costs are an important factor in strategic success. It is therefore essential to make a careful analysis and assessment of the company's cost structure. The best way of doing this is by analysing the individual value added stages in the company in comparison with competitors. Figure 4.3 gives an example of an analysis of this kind.

THE STRATEGY PURSUED BY THE COMPANY SO FAR

Every company has an idea of the direction it wants to move in and the way in which its

Fig 4.2 Capability analysis

1. Products and services

* Development of new products and services

* Improvements to products and services

* Offering a complete range of products and services

* Offering top quality

* Offering top after-sales service and assistance

2. Activities in the market

* Effective handling of existing and potential market segments

* Offering to solve customers' problems

* Opening new market segments

* Employing a successful sales force

* Optimal pricing

* Competent and effective advertising

3. Functional skills

* Building up an excellent image

* Producing and selling at favourable costs

* Using high-quality staff

* Acquiring funds

* Introducing management systems and assessing organizational structures

* Effective policy of co-operation agreements, participations and acquisitions

(continued)

Fig 4.2 Capability analysis (cont).

4. Potentials for synergy	* Solving customers' problems
	* Serving market segments
	* Distribution
	* Technology
	* Production
	* etc.
5. Existing resources for expansion	* Finance
	* Management
	* Personnel
	* Technological innovations
	* etc.

resources are to be allocated. These may be just ideas in the owner's head, or there may be extensive documentation on the strategy, but in any case a clear distinction needs to be drawn between these ideas or written documentation and what is actually going on. My own studies in companies have shown that there can be considerable discrepancies between them (Pümpin 1986).

A company cannot decide on a new strategy without looking at what it has been doing up to now, and this is an important part of information analysis.

How can the strategy pursued in the past be identified? One way is to analyse documentation. One could look at the minutes of the last quarter's meetings and make a list of the problems that received most intensive consideration. More important, one can establish how resources were allocated at these meetings or in other decisions.

Fig 4.3 Cost structure of Beauty Cosmetic SA.

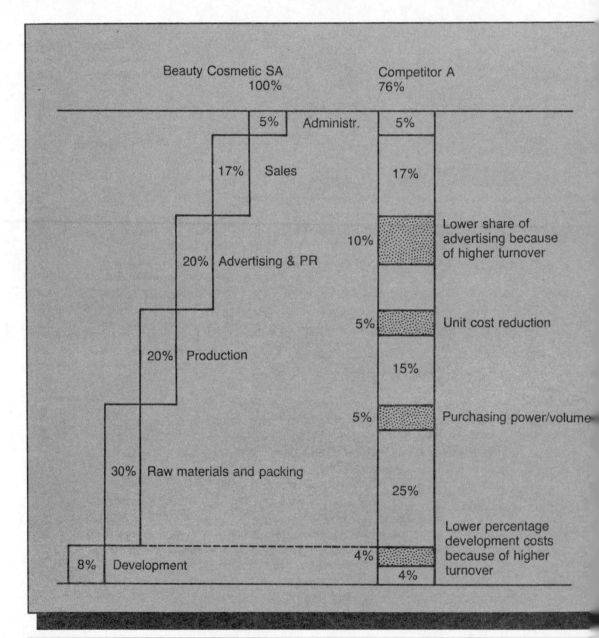

Secondly, management staff at various levels can be asked what strategy they were in effect pursuing. Finally, a very informative method is to use questionnaires at management meetings. I have found that a particularly good way of doing this is to show the strategy pursued so far in the form of a diagram with columns (see Figure 4.4). In this chart the length of the bars indicates the priority of the activity. In the example in Figure 4.4, in the past, customer consultation was of highest priority. Second were product quality and use of high technology. Some activities, such as innovation, were not pursued at all.

ANALYSIS OF THE CORPORATE CULTURE

The corporate culture includes the whole complex of opinions, norms and values that determine the attitude and behaviour of management and staff. It finds expression in the way the staff tackle and handle jobs (bureaucratically or very unconventionally, for example), in the basic attitudes to work (a high degree of intensity or unproductive attitude with a lot of fiddling around), in the attitude to customers (very helpful or uninterested) and many other aspects.

Recent research (e.g. Pümpin, 1984) has shown that the corporate culture has a strong influence on the company's performance. We also know that there is a close interrelation between the corporate culture and the company's strategy. It has been shown that the corporate culture exercises an influence when strategy is being developed. For example, in a highly cost-conscious company any strategic alternative that could not be exactly quantified was rejected straight away. The culture will also play an important part when the strategy is being implemented. A strategy that is not compatible with the corporate culture can only be implemented with great input, and

Fig 4.4 The strategy pursued in the past (insurance company).

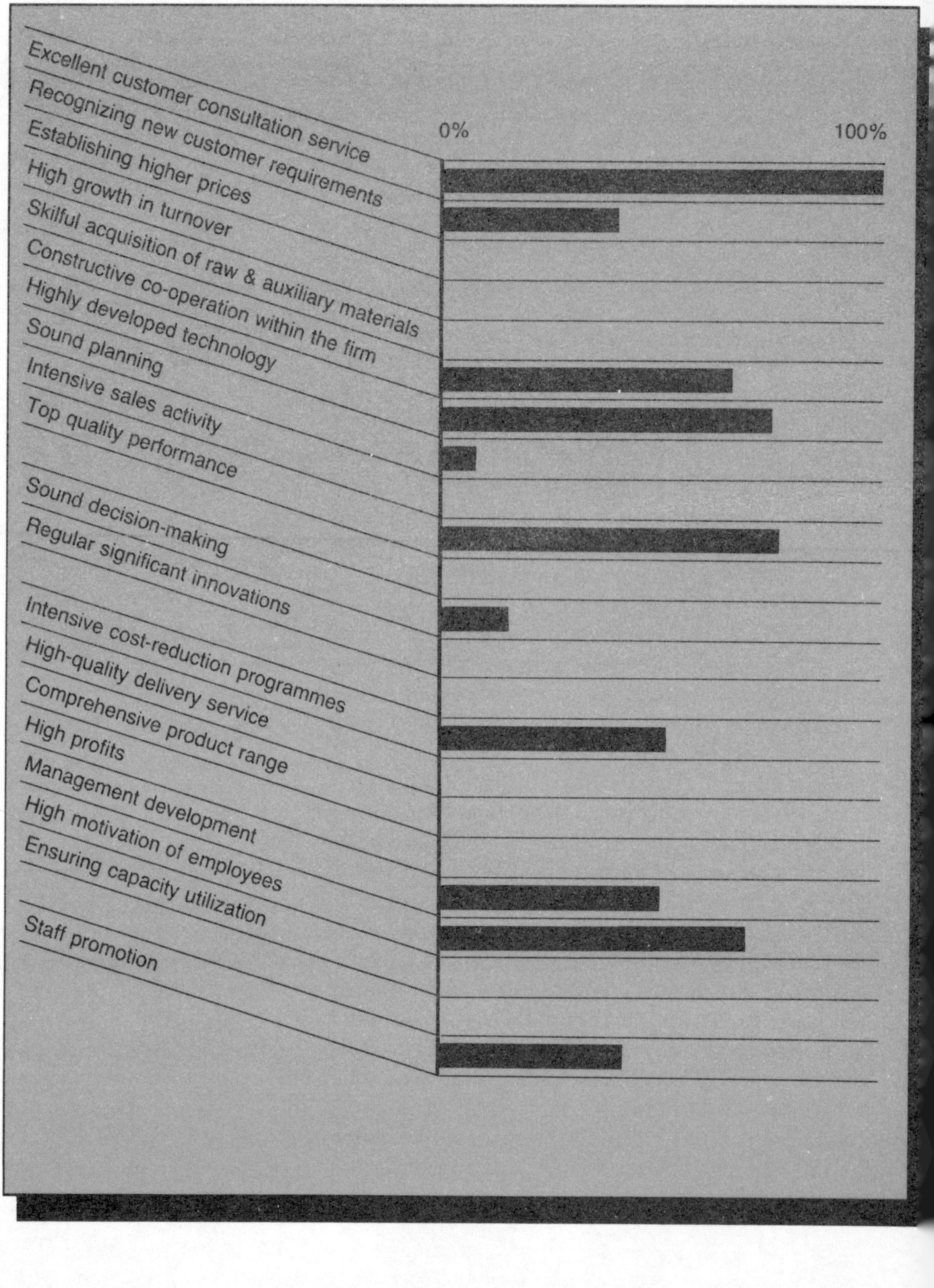

Excellent customer consultation service
Recognizing new customer requirements
Establishing higher prices
High growth in turnover
Skilful acquisition of raw & auxiliary materials
Constructive co-operation within the firm
Highly developed technology
Sound planning
Intensive sales activity
Top quality performance
Sound decision-making
Regular significant innovations
Intensive cost-reduction programmes
High-quality delivery service
Comprehensive product range
High profits
Management development
High motivation of employees
Ensuring capacity utilization
Staff promotion

0%   100%

very carefully planned social change may be required (see Law 10 of SEP Management).

What aspects of the corporate culture need to be taken into consideration? There are four general aspects:

* The strength of the corporate culture. The question here is whether the company has strongly developed cultural norms or whether these are indecisive.

* The consistency of the corporate culture. Are the cultures evident in different areas of the company compatible with each other?

* How far does the corporate culture match the strategy pursued up to now?

* The fundamental orientation of the corporate culture.

Seven points should be considered in identifying the orientation of the corporate culture:

1. Attitudes to customers: To what extent is the customer considered? Do the customer's interests always come first?

2. Attitudes to staff: Are they trusted? How about participation?

3. Attitudes to results and performance: What is the attitude to work and how target-oriented is the staff?

4. Attitudes to innovation: Is an innovative attitude promoted on principle? How frequent is innovation? Are mistakes through innovation activity tolerated?

5. Attitudes to costs: How important are costs? How often are economy drives and cost-reduction measures introduced?

6. Attitudes to the company: How loyal are the staff? Is there a community spirit? Do the employees identify with their firm?

7. Attitudes to technology: How important are production technology and materials technology in the firm? How important is technical progress?

The orientation can be shown in a diagram. Figure 4.5 gives three examples of different corporate cultures. In the metal processing firm cost-orientation predominates, while the services firm is more concerned with its customers.

There are many different ways of establishing what the corporate culture is. It can be identified in a very informal way through group discussions and by observing the way the management behaves. But there are also systematic analytical methods available in which the corporate culture is generally identified mainly through questionnaires supplemented by observation, documentary analysis and so on.

Environment analysis

The environment analysis should cover factors and trends outside the firm and here four areas can be distinguished:

* the general environment

* the industry or sector

* the market

* competitors

The main purpose of the environment analysis is to detect opportunities and threats, but also to judge the risks.

In certain fields a creative approach can be used to pinpoint new trends and changes. This applies for instance to the introduction of new technologies, new legal developments, etc. Other aspects, such as number of customers, competitor costs, etc., have to be analysed on the basis of detailed quantitative data.

Fig 4.5 The basic strategic orientation that determines the corporate culture.

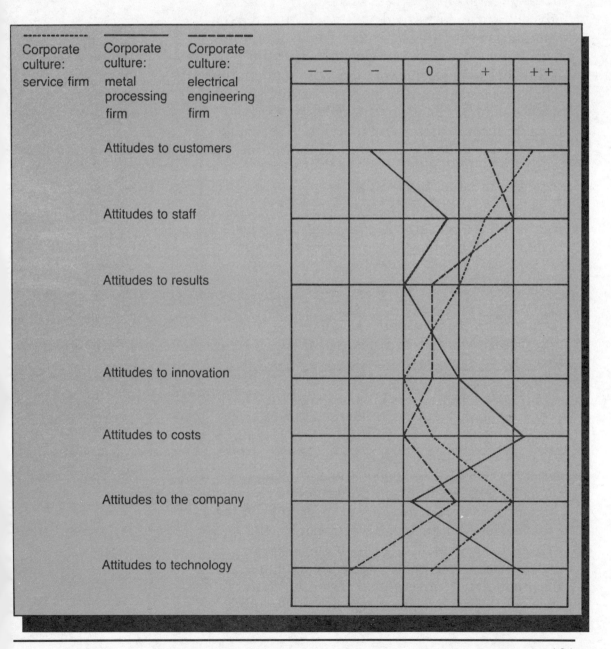

Corporate culture: service firm

Corporate culture: metal processing firm

Corporate culture: electrical engineering firm

	– –	–	0	+	+ +
Attitudes to customers					
Attitudes to staff					
Attitudes to results					
Attitudes to innovation					
Attitudes to costs					
Attitudes to the company					
Attitudes to technology					

GENERAL ENVIRONMENT ANALYSIS

The general environment analysis covers ecology, technology, the general economic situation, demographic and social or psychological trends and the political and legal situation.

In the general environment analysis it is advisable to make critical analyses of the areas of information that are particularly relevant for the firm. If, for instance, it is evident that, in the technological environment area, office automation will become strategically more important, careful studies should be made in this field. To get away from traditional patterns of thought it is sensible to use and include a wide range of information and opinions. Unprejudiced or neutral strategic consultants can be most valuable.

Figure 4.6 is a checklist of possible items to be included in the general environment analysis.

Trends in the environment can bring opportunities and entail risks for the firm. The introduction of a new material can create opportunities for new products, but it will constitute a danger if competitors can use it to displace the firm's products from the market. To clarify a situation of this kind, we need to go back to the company analysis. If the company has strongly developed capabilities that will enable it to respond then the new development will certainly constitute an opportunity, for the company will be better equipped than its competitors to make good use of the change. If the new development reveals a weak spot it will constitute a threat. (The introduction of the digital clock, for instance, was a great danger to the producers of conventional clocks, for their strength lay in analogue mechanisms. For other manufacturers, especially the Japanese, who had

Fig 4.6 General environment analysis.

Areas	Criteria

Ecological environment	* Availability of energy
	  – oil
	  – gas
	  – electricity
	  – coal
	  – other sources of energy
	* Availability of raw materials
	* Environment protection trends
	  – awareness of the environment
	  – pollution
	  – environment protection legislation
	* Recycling
	  – availability of recycleable material
	  – recycling costs

Technology	* Production technology
	  – development trends in process technology
	  – innovation potential
	  – automation/process control: use of microcomputers
	* Product innovation
	  – development trends in product technology
	    hardware
	    software
	  – innovation potential
	* Substitution technologies
	  – possible innovations
	  – cost trends
	* Recycling technology

The economy	* Trends in the national income in relevant countries
	* The development of international trades
	  – trade in goods
	  – economic integration
	  – protectionism
	* Trends in balance of payments and exchange rates
	* Expected inflation
	* Capital market developments
	* Developments in employment
	* Expected propensity to invest
	* Expected cyclical fluctuations
	  – frequency
	  – type
	* Developments in specific relevant economic sectors
	(continued)

Fig 4.6 General environment analysis (cont)

Areas	Criteria

Demographic and social or psychological trends	*Population development in relevant countries
	  – general
	  – in important groups of the population
	  – migration
	
	* Socio-psychological trends
	  – attitude to work
	  – propensity to save
	  – leisure patterns
	  – attitude to the business sector
	  – attitude to automation
	  – attitude to relevant materials
	  – attitude to relevant products

Politics and law	* Global political trends
	  – East– West
	  – North– South
	  – general danger of local or international conflicts
	  – market position of producers of raw materials
	
	* Political parties in relevant countries
	
	* Development trends in economic policy
	
	* Trends in social legislation and labour law
	
	* Importance and influence of trade unions
	
	* Scope for companies to act

considerable experience in electronics, it constituted a great opportunity.)

Companies do not generally get into difficulties because they have failed to make detailed analyses of their environment. The problem is rather that certain fundamental trends are not correctly assessed or recognized. The Atari company found itself in difficulties mainly because it had misinterpreted environmental trends: its global assessment of the receptivity of the market and the fashion trend in video games was incorrect. The difficulties experienced by Volkswagen at the end of the 1960s were not caused by a failure to make detailed analyses. The problem was that the technical obsolescence of the 'Beetle' was recognized too late as a fundamental problem.

For the general environment analysis this means that attention must be focused on a few central issues. It is therefore advisable to concentrate the initial broad analysis of the general environment. The result must be available in the form of a compressed account of a few opportunities and threats that are becoming evident in the environment.

INDUSTRY ANALYSIS

In principle the same considerations that were outlined for the general environment analysis apply to the industry analysis. The difference is that here the analysis is concentrated on the sector or industry relevant to the company.

Figure 4.7 shows the main points that could be of relevance and should be included in a sectoral analysis. Particularly important are the structure of the sector, the obstacles to the emergence of new competitors and the competitive situation (Porter, 1980). The information obtained orally needs to be analysed further to show what opportunities may be available to the firm and what the latent risks are.

MARKET ANALYSIS

The market analysis is of crucial importance and two aspects should be emphasized:

Fig 4.7 Industry analysis.

Main points	Analysis
Structure of the sector	Number of suppliers Heterogeneity of suppliers Types of supplier Organization of the sector (associations, agreements, etc.)
Structure of customers	Number of customers Types of customer
Employment situation and competition	Capacity utilization How fierce is the competition
Main competitive weapons	Quality Range Advice Price Delivery dates Etc.
Distribution structure	Geographical Sales channels
Nature of sector	General direction (materials, technology, customer problems, etc.)
Security	Barriers to the emergence of new customers Substitutability of product

* Firstly, the quantitative data relevant for the firm need to be collected. An estimate of the growth rate to be expected in future is particularly important as are the expected market volume and market share of individual competitors.

* Secondly, there are a number of qualitative aspects that need to be considered, and here we need to answer the following questions:

  – What are the requirements of the customers who buy the products?

  – How are these requirements now being met?

  – How, when and where do people buy?

  – How do customers obtain their information?

Figure 4.8 gives the appropriate breakdown of market data.

Fig 4.8 Market analysis.

Quantitative market data	Market volume Position in the product life cycle Degree of saturation Growth (quantity, in % p.a.) Market shares Stability of demand
Qualitative market data	Structure of customer requirements Motives for buying Buying processes/information behaviour Competitor's market strength

COMPETITION ANALYSIS

In the competition analysis every significant competitor should be subject to careful examination. In fragmented sectors with a large number of competitors (e.g. architecture, construction, hotels and catering) competitors can be considered in groups. It is particularly interesting to list the SEPs that competitors have occupied. Then potential new competitors need to be included in the analysis. There is a particular danger of the emergence of new competitors if:

* the sector is growing strongly.

* there is low investment intensity coupled with a medium to high market concentration.

* the sector is very profitable and market concentration is medium to high.

The criteria to be considered in the competition analyses are (for each competitor or group of main competitors):

* main capabilities (strengths) of the competitor

* main weaknesses

* Strategic Excellence Positions occupied

* recognizable strategies

* present position:

    – total turnover

    – turnover in relevant product groups

    – total market shares

    – market shares in relevant product groups

* product policy

* price situation

* cost structure

* profit situation

* financial strength

* main reasons for success or failure

From the overall competition analysis conclusions can be drawn. The areas in which competitors are vulnerable to attack can be listed, as can the points where competitors are strong.

STAKEHOLDER ANALYSIS

The purpose of every company is to fulfil the needs of its stakeholders. They may include:

* its shareholders

* its management

* its workforce

* its customers

* its suppliers

* its community

A sound strategy can be developed only if the needs and expectations of the stakeholders are understood. Therefore, this subject should be carefully discussed in the information analysis.

The purpose of the stakeholder analysis is to develop criteria that can be used to evaluate SEPs

and strategies. The analysis should consist of
answering, from the point of view of the
stakeholders, the following questions:

* How important is *differentiation* (quality,
  innovation, etc.)?

* What is the attitude to *cost reduction* and
  efficiency?

* What importance is attached to the *time factor*?
  Is great stress laid on quick, short-term results
  or is there a preference for long-term
  optimization?

* What are the stakeholders' ideas on the
  concentration of forces? Do they prefer a narrow
  strategy which concentrates forces fully or are
  they prepared to implement a broadly-based
  (diversified) strategy as well?

* What importance is attached to *concentrating
  on strengths,* or exploiting opportunities for
  synergy?

* What importance is attached to the *utilization
  of opportunities* and so *growth in turnover*?

* What is the stakeholders' attitude to the
  matching of aims with resources? Are they
  prepared to set high targets that bear the
  corresponding risks or are they looking for a
  more careful policy that will balance risks?
  What importance is attached to avoiding risks?

These eight questions correspond to the basic
rules of strategy discussed in the second chapter.
The object is to produce a list of the priorities the
stakeholders attach to each of these rules in
practice.

Of course, different categories of stakeholders often have conflicting interests. Nevertheless their priorities should be evaluated because they will be needed in the process of strategy evaluation.

Strategic analyses

When these analyses are complete all the information relevant for the development of a strategy should be available:

* the main capabilities (strengths) and weaknesses of the company and its cost structure, the strategy pursued up to now and the corporate culture

* the main development trends and opportunities in the general environment and any latent threats

* the main trends and opportunities or threats in the company's own industry

* the main trends, opportunities and risks in the company's own market

* the Strategic Excellence Positions occupied by competitors and their main strengths and weaknesses

* the requirements of the stakeholders.

The available data must now be evaluated for their relevance to the company's strategy, and here there are three tasks:

* Firstly, the success factors that will be relevant for the future activities of the firm need to be identified, together with the possible Strategic Excellence Positions they could give rise to.

* Even under the most difficult environmental

conditions a dynamic company can plan new ventures. These possibilities are extremely important in the offensive forward-looking concept of the SEP. For that reason the second task is to sift the information once more to see what possibilities there are for new activities.

* Finally the company's own strategic position can be planned, and here the key problems revealed by the information analysis need to be outlined and assessed.

IDENTIFYING THE SUCCESS FACTORS

In every environmental and market situation there are certain factors that are crucial for the success of a company. If, for instance, all the suppliers in a consumer goods market are offering goods of the same quality, success can depend on differences in price. In another case the success factor may be direct mail or the availability of the goods through a wide distribution network. These are mainly market-related factors. There may also be success factors in other areas of the environment. In a certain phase a company's success may depend on the possibilities of obtaining raw materials. In another it may be optimal relations to authorities and so on (see also Ohmae, 1982).

Clearly these success factors are related to Strategic Excellence Positions. The objective is to identify possible success factors and then develop SEPs related to them.

The strategic analyses should be made as follows:

1. Examine the environment, the sector and the market for possible success factors. A specific factor can be regarded as a success factor if business success largely depends on whether a company has particular capabilities for exploiting that factor.

2. The next step is to identify from the analysis of competitors what success factors they are already exploiting. That means that the Strategic Excellence Positions already occupied by competitors must be identified.

3. As we see from the strategic principles of differentiation and the indirect approach it is hardly advisable to make a frontal attack on competitors. That would be too expensive in comparison with the yield or return that could be expected and it would be better to consider Strategic Excellence Positions that competitors have not yet occupied. These can be considered as *possible Strategic Excellence Positions* for the company.

These then provide the alternatives to be discussed when the decision on the company's future strategy is being taken.

POSSIBILITIES FOR NEW ACTIVITIES

The general environment analysis, the sector analysis and the market analysis will reveal new fields of activity which the company could take up. New activities might be possible in any field of the company's operations. In one case there may be opportunities for new products or new markets, in another there may be new co-operation agreements, participations or acquisitions. But there may also be a possibility of using new sources of supply, new technologies, new sales channels and so on.

Since a medium-sized company may well find it can quickly identify 20 to 30 possible fields of activity there is a risk of some interesting avenues being overlooked. It is therefore advisable to go through the information analyses systematically with possible fields of activity in mind and enter these on a worksheet. The ideas on this worksheet

can be used in the development of the strategy and
they will serve as a valuable basis for the
discussion of alternatives.

KEY STRATEGIC PROBLEMS

The method of information analysis outlined here
serves as a comprehensive assessment of the
company's position. It should also indicate critical
problem areas. How can key strategic problems be
recognized and assessed?

The starting point is the analysis of the company
and its environment. Of particular importance
here are the capability analysis, the analysis of
the cost structure, the opportunities and threats
evident in the general environment analysis and
in the sector analysis and finally the expected
development in turnover indicated by the market
analysis.

To identify the key strategic problems the
information analyses have to be examined point
by point, asking whether *strategic action* should
be taken in that particular situation. If so, this
should be entered in a list of key strategic
problems.

It will be clear that most key strategic problems
will emerge

* where the company has particular capabilities
  that are not yet adequately utilized

* where specific opportunities are evident in the
  analysis of the environment, the sector, the
  market or competitors' positions.

It is best to concentrate first and foremost on the
positive aspect of problems, such as capabilities
that could be further utilized or opportunities that
are becoming evident. Of course, weaknesses and

threats must be acknowledged but the problems should not be seen only in a negative light. The key strategic problems can be assessed to show their importance for the company as a whole and how urgent they are.

Organizing the information analysis

The analysis phase should be organized so that a strategy can be decided on that is effective and can be put into practice quickly. This will only be possible if the entire management identifies with the strategy, and the information analysis should therefore be organized so that the main steps can be worked out by a team of the appropriate staff. It is of crucial importance to win over all managers to the new strategy and the following method has proved its worth in practice (see also Figure 4.9).

The process of planning a strategy should begin with an initial meeting. This should last about a day and be used to familiarize the management with the strategic approach and the concept of strategic management. At this meeting steps can be taken to start the information analysis. The main concern should be to establish the areas that are most important for the company. Individual managers can be allocated specific tasks for the detailed analysis and their responsibilities laid down. An external consultant can play a valuable part in a meeting of this kind as neutral director or critical observer.

Following the initial meeting small teams or individuals should set about gathering the specific items of information. The relevant data should be available after a few weeks. A second meeting can then be held in which the material is discussed by the management group. The first assessments can now be made of the strategic position occupied by the company so far and its main capabilities, its cost structure in comparison to its competitors, the strategy pursued so far and the corporate culture. The environment analysis can also be evaluated.

Beside these assessments, this meeting, which again should last a day, will involve intensive discussion of the strategic information, which will probably reveal further gaps in data showing where more research is needed. This further research again will generally take a few weeks.

One of the main purposes of these meetings is to ensure that the results obtained are put into practice within a certain period of time, and for that reason it is extremely important to initiate specific actions designed to improve the company's performance at the end of each of them. Can that be done while the information analysis is going on? The answer is certainly yes.

All information analysis yields insight and recognition which does not need lengthy theoretical argument or to be formulated as a strategy to take effect. If, for instance, it emerges in the course of the information analysis that the quality of a group of products is inadequate the firm does not need to wait to do something about it. It can start straight away on a quality improvement programme. Even if quality never becomes a Strategic Excellence Position the measures themselves and any improvement achieved in the products or the company's performance will be bound to have a positive effect on its image.

Experience has shown that the following fields of activity are particularly suited to short-term action

Fig 4.9 The organization of information analysis.

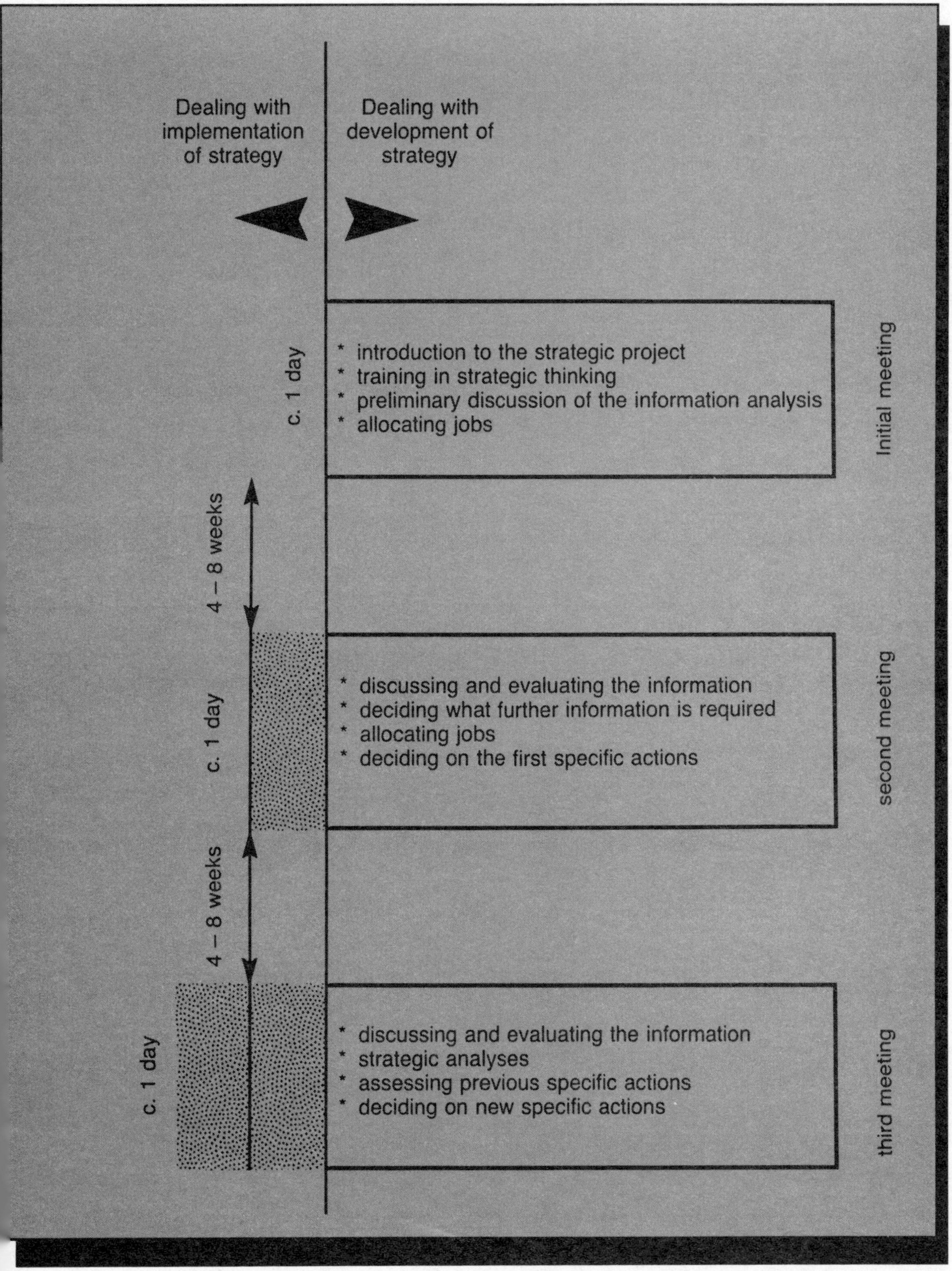

Dealing with implementation of strategy

Dealing with development of strategy

c. 1 day

* introduction to the strategic project
* training in strategic thinking
* preliminary discussion of the information analysis
* allocating jobs

Initial meeting

4 – 8 weeks

c. 1 day

* discussing and evaluating the information
* deciding what further information is required
* allocating jobs
* deciding on the first specific actions

second meeting

4 – 8 weeks

c. 1 day

* discussing and evaluating the information
* strategic analyses
* assessing previous specific actions
* deciding on new specific actions

third meeting

programmes that derive directly from the information analysis:

* improvements in attitudes to customers (more attention to customer requirements, better service, improvements in quality, looking after customers better)

* better innovation capability (more entrepreneurship in the approach, more flexibility, better methods of developing and introducing products)

* higher productivity (value analyses of products and administration, cost reduction programmes)

* better attitudes toward the staff (new incentive systems, measures to improve the corporate culture, team formation, personal targets and programmes to achieve these).

Information for the staff and staff training will play a very important part in all these short-term measures. These short-term measures will not only save time, they will also improve staff motivation and create more enthusiasm. Rapid and concrete action after meetings of this nature is a visible testimony to the decisiveness and initiative of the management. New actions should therefore always be started within a few days, if not on the very next day after the meeting. Otherwise the new enthusiasm will soon evaporate!

After the second meeting groups or individuals should set about making the more detailed analyses that are known to be needed. The results can be discussed a few weeks later in a third meeting, when the team can proceed to the strategic analyses. Again specific improvement measures should be introduced; the actions started after the second meeting can be discussed and any results obtained in the interval assessed. But, most important, the third meeting will yield a full information analysis, and this is the basis for the actual development of the strategy.

The 'grand strategy'

The basic document in which the strategy of a company or a large organization (or organizational unit) is written is called 'its grand strategy' and it contains the fundamental decisions of the organization. It makes clear the overall long-term direction that is intended for the company.

Many companies already produce extensive strategy documents which too often end up in a desk drawer and are never applied, simply because they are so comprehensive.

A concentrated document can be kept in mind much more easily. This is very helpful in daily management, where it is not possible to consult written documents all the time.

The more concise and concentrated the documentation, the clearer will be the aims of the strategy. Short, precise declarations require much more decisiveness and courage than extensive documentation. The statement, 'We intend to promote product A intensively' is clear and binding, while 'We want to promote product A, but at the same time we do not want to overlook products B and C, so that a certain amount of attention will be directed to product C as customers . . . etc.' is long-winded and imprecise.

For these reasons it is strongly suggested that the grand strategy should never exceed a few pages. In practice the most convenient length seems to be 4 to 6 pages.

Figure 4.10 shows the structure of a grand strategy. It contains the following elements:

A: THE VISION

There is one common characteristic in which all leaders excel: they have a vision of the future state of their organization (see e.g. the important findings of Bennis and Nanus, 1985).

This vision is the central concept for the future development of the company. It could be: 'World leader in fastening systems in the building industry', or 'European leader in aluminium processing', or 'Problem-solver for computerization in banking'.

The vision is the declaration of intent and is closely related to the Strategic Excellence Positions that are to be developed.

Fig 4.10 The structure of a grand strategy.

A: Vision

B: Strategic Excellence Positions
    Primary SEP
    Secondary SEPs

C: Product market objectives, other objectives
    1. Products
    2. Markets/market segments
    3. Production
    4. Growth
    5. Financial

D: Strategies for business functions and culture
    1. Innovation/R&D
    2. Marketing
    3. Production
    4. Profit, costs, finance
    5. Staff
    6. Management and organization
    7. Co-operation agreements, joint ventures, acquisitions
    8. Culture

E: Movements over time/timing

B: STRATEGIC EXCELLENCE POSITIONS (SEPs)

The central elements of the grand strategy are the Strategic Excellence Positions. They define the fields of activity in which the company intends to develop strategic superiority, i.e. the ways in which it is going to beat its competitors.

Remember that:

* SEPs can be product-related, market-related or function-related.

* The number of SEPs that can be developed is limited. This means that a company cannot decide on ten different SEPs. Ideally, the aim should be not more than two or three. In exceptional cases up to five can be chosen.

* The SEPs have to be of great value over as long a period in the future as possible.

* The SEPs should harmonize with each other.

* If possible they should build on strengths the company already has.

C: PRODUCT MARKET OBJECTIVES

This section of the grand strategy describes the objectives for products and markets and the priorities to be accorded to building up or reducing individual products or markets. Markets can be either geographical areas, sectors or market segments. 'Products' does not just mean physical goods, it can mean solutions to customers' problems or procedures and systems which combine hardware and software.

The product/market objectives define the company's market share and growth rate targets.

In this section also other objectives – e.g. profit objectives – may be established.

D: STRATEGIES FOR FUNCTIONS AND CULTURE

All the statements in the grand strategy concerning company functions and culture flow from the vision and the Strategic Excellence Positions desired, and they show the consequences these will have for the various areas of the company's activities, such as:

* innovation (R&D)

* marketing

* production

* profits, costs and finance

* staff

* management and organization

* co-operation agreements, joint ventures and acquisitions

* corporate culture

E: MOVEMENTS OVER TIME/TIMING

In what is now often a turbulent business and market situation it is extremely important to get the timing right. The management needs to decide in its basic strategy the sequence and timing of the large-scale strategic changes.

Figure 4.11 is an example of a basic strategy document developed for a French cosmetic firm.

Fig 4.11 Example of a basic strategy.

Beauty Cosmetic SA, Paris

A: VISION

Leading consultant to dealers in Europe in cosmetics for the sensitive skin

B: SEPs TO BE BUILT UP

1. Ability to service specialized dealers with a staff of highly trained consultants in a way that is clearly superior to competitors.
2. Optimal high-quality products to meet demand for beauty care and hygiene, especially for the sensitive skin.
3. Building up a style of communication that is informative in a positive emotional environment.

C: PRODUCT/MARKET OBJECTIVES/PRIORITIES; OTHER OBJECTIVES

1. Range

To be strongly promoted:	Skin-care products, protective and decorative cosmetics achieve x in turnover by ...
To be promoted:	Perfumes and toilet waters achieve y in turnover by ...
To be maintained:	Fashion accessories
To be reduced:	Products on commission for department Stores

2. Markets

a Geographical

To be strongly promoted:	F; D; CH: will produce 60% of turnover by 19..
To be promoted:	GB; Benelux
To be maintained:	USA, rest of Europe
To be reduced:	South America

b Demographic

To be strongly promoted:	Age group 30 – 50
To be promoted:	Age group over 50

c Psychological

To be strongly promoted:	Market segment 'the well-groomed woman/man'

d Purchasing power

To be strongly promoted:	Upper purchasing power groups

3. Market Position Objectives

Market share in countries F, CH and D: among top three suppliers to perfume dealers, drug stores, chemists and leading department stores (over 15% in each country).

(continued)

Fig 4.11 Example of a basic strategy (cont).

4. Growth Objectives
   * at least 12% p.a.
   * with due regard for sound financial conditions.

5. Profit Objectives
   Profit objective = 20% after taxes

D: FUNCTIONAL STRATEGIES
   1. Innovation
      Developing at least five new or new-style products p.a. in skin care.
      Developing new training systems for specialized dealers.

   2. Marketing
   a Product policy
      Up-to-date range limited to a few main products; excellent quality; new products only come on to the market when they are chemically and technically mature.
      Packing must match up to the quality of the products aesthetically and functionally.

   b Price policy
      Above medium price

   c Sales
      Priority to intensive contact with specialized dealers; biggest customers are visited twice a month; sales staff selected using requirement profiles; constant further training in knowledge and sales techniques.

   d Communication
      Concentrate on the image 'quality leader, specializing in the sensitive skin'.
      Advertising mainly informative. Main vehicle: print media.
      Regular PR with product and company information.

   e Distribution
      To order: delivery within 24 hours.

   3. Production
      Production plant: always using the latest technology to ensure quality.
      Purchase products in the decorative field.
      Centralize production in X.
      Buying maxims: use high-quality raw materials and packaging.

   4. Profits, Costs and Finance
      Profits after tax should be 20% of turnover.
      Strict control of distribution costs.
      Financing must not infringe company's independence.

(continued)

Fig 4.11 Example of a basic strategy (cont).

5. Staff

Highly qualified and motivated; full identification with their jobs and the company's goals.

6. Management and Organization

Flexible organization; the greatest possible scope for staff.

7. Joint Ventures, Mergers and Acquisitions

Close co-operation with specialized dealers' organizations and specialists in communication.

Joint venture in decorative cosmetics.

Acquire a small chain of specialized dealers to give direct contact with customers.

8. Culture

Building a strong market and dealer-oriented culture.

E: MOVEMENT OVER TIME

Build up training system within 12 months.
Expand distribution in CH and GB rapidly.

The philosophy behind the approach outlined here can be characterized as follows:

* *Clarity of aim*
The Strategic Excellence Positions desired must be clearly identified and the main idea they give rise to precisely formulated.

* *Harmonizing all the business activities*
Products, markets and company functions should be co-ordinated and made relevant to the SEP and the basic idea. The key question is: How must function Z be carried out in order to develop A as an SEP? For example, What will be the effect on our personnel policy if we want to build up 'Quality' as a primary SEP?

* *Concentration*
Clear focal points must be formed in regard to the SEP and products and markets.

The emphasis on focusing and concentration means that the SEP philosophy is generally incompatible with the diversification favoured by the portfolio management approach to business. Although that approach can certainly help to clarify matters during an information analysis, it should never be used mechanistically when the strategy is being decided. Diversified strategies make it very difficult to achieve *unité de doctrine* and the necessary strategic thrust. These are extremely important psychological elements, and a company can only make successful use of them if it achieves a harmonious, co-ordinated and coherent orientation. The basic strategy is an essential foundation for this.

Choosing the strategic direction

Even a concentrated grand strategy usually contains a considerable number of individual product, market and functional strategy points. If the new strategy is to be successfully implemented it is vital to guard against diluting efforts in numerous unco-ordinated or, even worse, contradictory goals.

It is therefore essential that the strategy statement should establish a single 'strategic direction' to underpin the individual strategy points and provide unity of purpose for managers required to implement the plan.

The types of generic strategy available are well documented in business literature notably by Professor Porter of Harvard in his book, *Competitive Strategy* (Porter, 1980).

The following paragraphs are confined to brief summaries of the main options available, and to an indication of the types of SEPs appropriate to each.

Competitive superiority

Let us first look at the strategies that can be deduced from the three ways of differentiation, low costs and timing.

DIFFERENTIATION

The main strategic concern in differentiation is to mark the company off from its competitors as far as possible. The first aim is to achieve optimal satisfaction of customer requirements, so customer orientation is closely bound up with differentiation.

The main feature of differentiation strategies is that forces are concentrated on market-oriented SEPs. Possible differentiation strategies include the development of the following SEPs:

* 'quality'

* 'product range'

* 'image'

* 'advice to customers'

* 'sales'

* 'distribution'

* 'innovation'

COSTS

In this case the strategic direction is mainly towards achieving favourable unit costs (for example by concentrating on cost reduction as an

SEP). But efforts could also be directed to building up productivity generally as an SEP.

A COMBINATION OF DIFFERENTIATION AND COST REDUCTION

The third possible strategic direction would be to aim for both maximum differentiation and optimal unit costs. This means building up SEPs in both differentiation and cost reduction.

TIMING

A fourth possible strategic direction focuses on the timing factors. Here the company concentrates on creating structures that will enable optimal movement over time. Strategies of this kind could include developing these SEPs:

* 'ability to develop products rapidly and introduce them to the market'.

* 'quickly copying competitors' innovations'.

* 'flexibility' (ability to adjust rapidly to changes in environment conditions).

Product- and market-related strategies

The product/market matrix in Figure 4.12 shows that there are four possible market-related strategic directions.

MARKET PENETRATION

* *Intensifying market penetration*. The main idea of the basic strategy is to exploit existing markets more intensively. The company concentrates on what it has been offering up to now.

* *Relaunch*. Existing products are made more attractive by 'relaunching' them.

* *Imitation.* Competitor's products are imitated. The company specializes in successfully launching 'me-too' products.

* *Cost and price reductions.* Efforts are concentrated on lowering costs and so lowering prices. Often the main focus is on value analysis and the development of new processes.

* *Unbundling.* With growing market maturity the need can arise to fragment systems or solutions to problems that have been in use up to now and offer the individual elements separately.

Fig 4.12 The product/market matrix.

	Current products	New products
Current markets	Market penetration	Market development
New markets	Product development	Diversification

MARKET DEVELOPMENT

* Opening up new markets.

* Acquiring new classes of customer.

* Using new distribution channels.

* New applications – a strategy centred on finding new uses for existing products.

PRODUCT DEVELOPMENT

* New products

* New product lines

* New services

* New systems and solutions to problems for firms that only supply hardware; offering more comprehensive solutions to problems may be an interesting avenue.

DIVERSIFICATION

Offering new products for new markets is generally considered extremely costly. As many conglomerates have discovered it is a high-risk strategy. The problem is that it is very difficult to build up new SEPs through diversification.

Synergy-related strategies

A further way of defining the strategic direction is to indicate the synergies that are to be utilized, which gives three main types of strategy:

MATERIALS-ORIENTED STRATEGIES

The strategic direction is based on offering all the products (generally for different groups of customers) that can be produced with the same material (e.g. aluminium). The aim is to build up an SEP in processing that material.

TECHNOLOGY-ORIENTED STRATEGIES

The strategic direction is based on offering all the products (generally for different groups of customers) that can be produced in the same plant (e.g. by drop-forgings). The aim here is to build up an SEP in the corresponding production technology.

MARKET-ORIENTED STRATEGIES
The strategic direction is based on offering every product required by a specific group of customers, for example, producing and selling all the products that skiers need. The aim is then to build up an SEP in knowing the requirements of this group of customers, perhaps working in co-operation with some of them.

Integration strategies

Finally, the company can try to improve its competitive position through forward or backward integration:

FORWARD INTEGRATION
The purpose of forward integration is generally to open up or create new groups of customers and secure their loyalty. It often entails developing new market-related SEPs.

BACKWARD INTEGRATION
There are generally two purposes to backward integration: first to build up an SEP in the field of favourable materials acquisition by opening up new sources of supply. The central factor, however, may be cost considerations, and the backward integration may be intended to strengthen the company's cost competitiveness. Here then the aim would be to build up an SEP in cost structures.

It will be seen that any company faces a considerable array of strategic options. However, if the information analysis has been sufficiently vigorous then the options can usually be reduced fairly rapidly to a limited set of interesting possibilities that deserve detailed consideration.

The next section describes how to choose among the most promising possibilities.

How to formulate a strategy

In a few instances, depending upon the material emerging from the information analysis, straightforward logic and deduction may be all that are required to decide on a strategic direction.

Such a painless decision-making process may sound attractive, particularly to senior managers facing agonizing choices about future strategy. In practice, however, it also entails two very considerable disadvantages.

* There is a risk that other, perhaps even more advantageous, alternatives could be overlooked. Pure logic leaves little scope for creativity.

* Critical managers are inclined to keep questioning the grand strategy, even when it appears to have been agreed. If a range of alternatives has been evolved and systematically evaluated the choice of the grand strategy will be much more firmly founded. Later, objections will only be considered if they contain really new suggestions that were not discussed when the various alternatives were being assessed.

For this reason the management team responsible for developing strategy should ensure that all the various options are fully examined and discussed. To do this they must go back to the 'success factors' and 'possible SEPs' that were noted during the strategic analyses. A rough assessment of these possibilities should be made following the strategic principles. Unsuitable SEPs can be eliminated. Those that remain (usually not less than three but not more than seven) are developed into *alternative grand strategies* by

* first formulating the *vision* of the strategy and the related SEPs.

* defining the product and market priorities and objectives that correspond to the vision and the SEPs.

* deciding on functional and cultural strategies that promote the SEPs.

* defining principles for the timing of changes.

It is not necessary at this stage to work out the alternative basic strategies in detail. A brief, concentrated account covering about one page is enough for the assessment.

At the end of this stage the company should have a set of three to seven alternative, roughly-conceived grand strategies. Each of them should generally have a different strategic direction and so a different philosophy.

The management must then undertake a very careful assessment of these different grand strategies and the one that seems best should be worked out in more detail as the one the company is to follow.

As has been stressed throughout this book, we are not just aiming to find the strategy that seems to hold most potential for success, we also need to take psychological and social factors into account and we should therefore choose an evaluation method that enables the management to agree objectives and unite in pursuing the chosen strategy. The evaluation method should be simple and suited for group discussion. It should exclude conflict of interest wherever possible and it should also help the management and staff to identify with the approach and direction that have been chosen.

What are the criteria for assessing the success potential of a strategy? Taking the strategic principles and basic rules of strategy in Chapter 1 of this book as evaluation criteria, the following questions have to be asked:

* *Differentiation*. To what extent does the strategy permit differentiation from competitors?

* *Efficiency*. To what extent does the strategy lead to favourable unit costs, high value added or low investment intensity?

* *Timing*. What time advantages are entailed in the strategy? Does it enable Strategic Excellence Positions to be occupied ahead of competitors?

* *Concentration of forces*. To what extent are forces concentrated with the strategy? Can it be implemented with an indirect approach?

* *Concentration on strengths and exploitation of synergy*. To what extent does the strategy rely on available strengths? What synergies can be utilized? How about avoiding weaknesses?

* *Utilizing environmental opportunities*. To what extent will the strategy enable environmental opportunities to be utilized and threats to be avoided?

* *Matching aims with resources, avoiding risks*. Can the strategy be implemented with the resources available? How great is the probability of success?

* *Unité de doctrine.* Will the strategy motivate the staff and win their enthusiastic support? Will it produce unity of purpose?

A scoring system can be used to evaluate alternative strategies (see Figure 4.13).

It must be stressed, however, that the main focus is not on allocating points, because subjective elements can never be entirely excluded. The overall process of thought which the discussions on the various criteria provoke is much more important. These discussions should be intensive and should give greater insight into the strategic problems the company is facing. This insight will be of the greatest value in forming attitudes and in building

Fig 4.13 Evaluation of alternative grand strategies through scoring.

Criteria	W	Alternative 1		Alternative 2		Alternative 3	
		D	W×D	W	W×D	W	W×D
1. Differentiation	5	5	25	3	15	4	20
2. Cost structure	2	3	6	5	10	2	6
3. Time	2	3	6	5	10	4	8
4. Concentration of forces	3	5	15	2	6	4	12
5. Concentration on strengths	4	3	12	4	16	3	12
6. Utilizing environmental opportunities	5	5	15	1	5	3	15
7. Matching aims with resources/avoiding risks	3	3	9	5	15	5	15
8. Unité de doctrine	4	5	20	1	4	4	16
			108		81		104

W=Weight   D=Degree of achievement

up understanding in depth of the way the individual strategies will work.

In this connection it is also advisable to refer to the key strategic problems set out in the information analysis in order to see how far the strategies being evaluated would enable them to be solved.

Considering the different basic strategies in more detail often enables them to be enriched.

* New main ideas and other possible primary SEPs emerge, so that further grand strategies can be formulated and included in the evaluation.

* It often becomes evident that there might be further possibilities in combinations of the individual grand strategies. In this case, too, the appropriate (combined) new grand strategy should be developed and assessed.

* In the course of the discussion the management will discover gaps in the information which have to be filled.

The method of evaluation outlined here should obviously be used flexibly. The data acquired during the information analysis are referred to continually but the basic business decision on the strategy should never result from a mechanistic allocation of points. Finding the right solution requires intuition and personal engagement as well as the formalized evaluation methods discussed here.

Once a particular alternative is chosen, the grand strategy can be outlined to produce the final strategy document, like the one in Figure 4.11.

The overall strategy development process is summarized in Figure 4.14.

Fig 4.14 Method of developing a grand strategy.

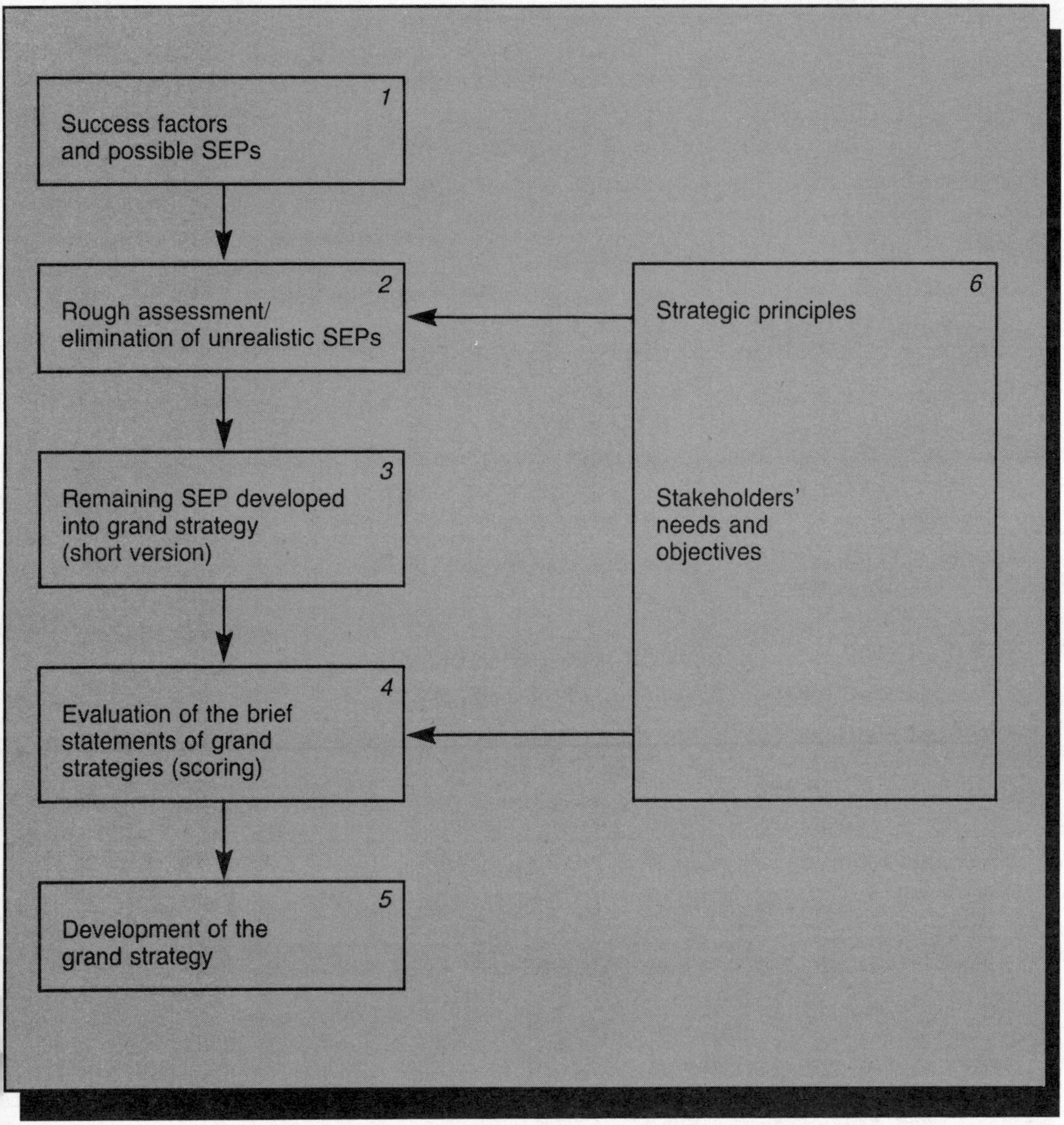

Organizing the process of formulating the strategy

From what has been said in this chapter it will be clear that the process of formulating the grand strategy must be handled by a management team. The best approach will be to organize workshops. An experienced consultant can usually enable the team to get through the work in a few days.

At the first workshop the possible SEPs and alternative visions should be discussed and roughly evaluated. Generally it is possible at this stage to outline alternative grand strategies as well. At the end of the workshop the management should be able to identify specific measures and actions which they can initiate straight away. Further detailed analyses may be needed and the appropriate persons should be instructed to carry them out.

In subsequent workshops what has been done in the meantime should be discussed. The main task is then to assess the alternatives. If the results are clear the team can proceed directly to outlining the definitive grand strategy.

The conclusion of the process of developing the strategy is a *fully formulated grand strategy*. This should take account of the environment and the company's position across a broad front and so provide the basis for successful business in future. But the social process involved in developing the strategy should not be underestimated. The discussions in the workshop should yield greater understanding in depth of the company's activities together with a more comprehensive view of the environment and the company, and the importance of this in creating *unité de doctrine* cannot be stressed strongly enough.

5 Achieving strategic thrust

In the past some companies have been disappointed with their strategic planning. They produce elaborate strategy documents stating comprehensive plans but years later find they are not putting the plans into practice. This is often because they fail to think through, in a systematic way, what is needed to *implement* the chosen strategy. One of the most important advantages of the SEP concept is that it facilitates implementation of the strategic plan, by focusing on a small, manageable number of priorities.

A step ahead in implementation

The traditional approach to strategy implementation is to develop an action plan for each new task and assume that the company will then operate in accordance with the new strategy. In reality the result is different. Each organizational unit interprets the strategy from its own point of view and this leads to unco-ordinated actions (see Figure 5.1).

When the SEP concept is applied three aspects must be taken into consideration:

* Generally a new grand strategy defines a new
  strategic direction which means change for the
  company, and change is usually resisted. The
  resistance can only be overcome if all forces are
  concentrated on the focal point where change is
  desired.

* Secondly, the company intends to achieve
  strategic superiority in fields of activity crucial to
  its future success. The Laws of SEP Management
  (especially Laws 4 and 7) predict that the number
  of fields of activity in which SEPs can be
  developed is very limited. It is only by
  concentrating on a few SEPs that a company may
  achieve true strategic superiority.

*Fig 5.1 Unco-ordinated actions as
they can often be seen in companies
with conventional strategy
approaches.*

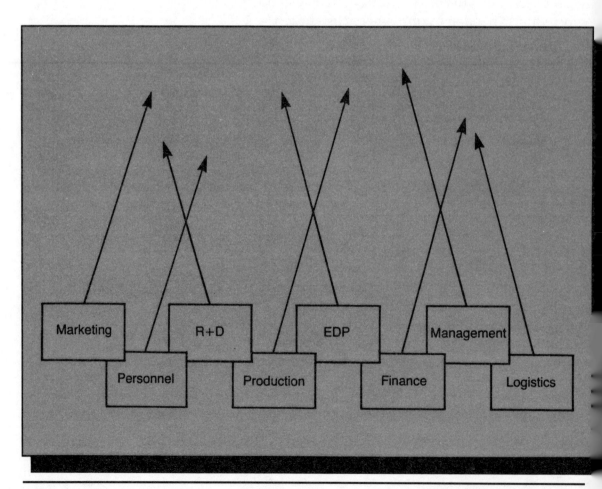

* Thirdly, it is desirable to gain momentum. The
company is generating strategic thrust and
therefore needs motivation and enthusiasm. If
business activities are performed mechanically,
nobody will be excited. But concentration on a few
key factors may change this. People can then
realize what they are working for and will work
with new energy.

These are the reasons why SEPs are needed. They
provide an opportunity to focus all company
activities on a few factors (see Figure 5.2).

Strategy is implemented in two ways:

* By the well-known management techniques, such

Fig 5.2 The key idea of the SEP
concept: all the company's activities
are angled towards the SEP. This
creates a concave effect and
stronger forces are released.

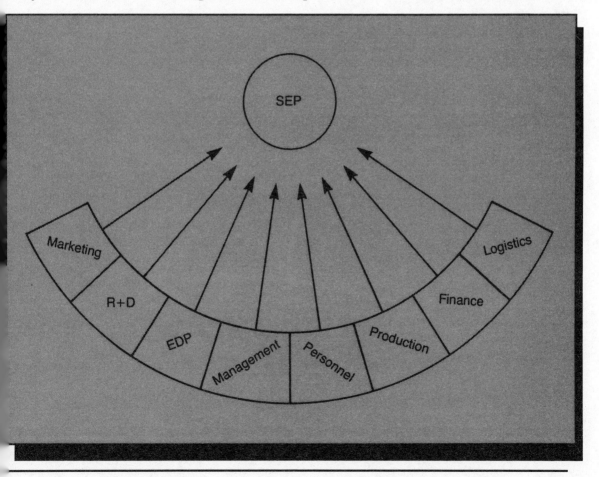

as plans, budgets, management systems and so on. These systems are quantitative: they have a sound logical basis. They are the *direct means* of strategy implementation.

* Secondly, by more qualitative activities, such as shaping the corporate culture, training, motivation etc. These techniques are the *indirect means* of strategy implementation.

This section examines both direct and indirect means and what they can contribute to that most elusive and demanding of goals – effective implementation.

Direct means of strategy implementation

Action plans

Every statement in the new basic strategy can be regarded as a definition of something that ought to be achieved in the future. This needs to be compared with the present state and the differences listed to show where the new strategy deviates from the present position.

If there are a large number of differences there is a great danger of releasing what may be called 'shock waves'. This happens if too many new measures are initiated at once. A large number of new tasks will then be embarked on but only a few of them will be consistently carried through. It is therefore important to set clear priorities and here there are two criteria we need to bear in mind:

* the importance of the measures for developing the SEP.

* how urgent the measures are.

Figure 5.3 shows differences weighted according to these criteria.

Fig 5.3 Sample list of weighted differences.

Differences between desired and present states	Importance for desired SEP	Degree of urgency
Introduction of product A	high	high
More intensive exploitation of German market	high	high
More intensive exploitation of GB market	medium	low
Build-up of agencies in Australia	medium	medium
New partner in acquiring raw material X	medium	high
In quality control: achieve 0.5% fault rate	high	high
Extended range of special products	medium	medium
Development of information material	high	high

The differences can now be arranged in order of priority. Clearly the problems that are shown to have high importance or urgency must be tackled first.

At the same time the responsibilities for handling the appropriate problems can be allocated and here use can be made of what is known as the 'Eisenhower Grid' (Figure 5.4):

* Tasks that are very important and very urgent should be tackled immediately under the direction of the top management.

* Tasks that are very urgent but only of medium to low importance can be delegated to the appropriate staff departments or other groups.

* Tasks that are very important but rated of medium or low urgency can be postponed until later.

Fig 5.4 The Eisenhower Grid: handling problems according to their importance and urgency.

		Urgency	
		High	Low
Importance	High	Treatment by top management	Schedule for treatment at a later date
	Low	Delegation	File (waste paper basket)

* Tasks that are not of high importance or urgency can be left aside, for the present.

Planning and budgeting

All effective management needs clear planning and budgeting. In the SEP concept of strategic management the following guidelines should be observed:

1. A new strategy should only be implemented if, when it is quantified, it shows profits which meet the requirements of the management and make optimal use of the possibilities in the environment. A concentrated *five-year plan* therefore needs to be drawn up. It shows and *quantifies* not only the company's activities up to now but also the new activities that the strategy will give rise to. The planning horizon needs to be widened or narrowed according to the company's situation and the nature of the strategy. The five-year plan must include the resources needed to build up the Strategic Excellence Positions and implement the grand strategy. It will also contain the appropriate calculations.

If the quantification shows that the returns from the strategy are inadequate, the management should subject the grand strategy it has chosen to a renewed and detailed examination and if necessary consider alternatives.

2. Of course the implementation of the strategy must be reflected in the *planning and budgeting for the year*. A clear grand strategy will make it possible to keep the plans simple. Again the focus must be on the Strategic Excellence Positions that are to be developed. Planning expenditure and effort may be reduced by abandoning annual planning where it is not really necessary – perhaps plans for a two-year period would be better.

Management systems

The information analysis in a capital goods firm showed that there were genuine opportunities for profit in large-scale systems. The management therefore decided to build up a strong SEP in this field and considerable resources were invested for that purpose in R&D.

But the introduction of the new products was extremely slow. An investigation showed that the subsidiaries and particularly their sales staff were still concentrating on selling small and medium-sized systems. The reason was that both the management of the subsidiaries and the sales staff got their bonuses on the basis of their annual turnover. It generally took more than one year to sell a large-scale system, so that switching the programme would have involved an unacceptable loss of income to them. It was not until the bonus system was adjusted (which took three years) that the firm was able to increase its turnover in large-scale systems.

This example shows that it is only possible to implement a strategy effectively if the management systems – in this case the method of allocating bonuses – are in tune with the new strategy.

THE SALARY AND BENEFITS SYSTEM

Many firms treat these as two separate and distinct fields. They use highly formalized salary systems, while non-financial remuneration is very marginal and handled quite informally. But this weakens the motivating force of the non-financial element. In view of the need to generate strategic drive it is better to treat financial and non-financial remuneration in the same way, since both will act as motivating forces.

The following guidelines are suggested for the use of remuneration systems in implementing a grand strategy:

* The remuneration must be consistently designed to reward behaviour that is *in line with the strategy*. Successful strategic behaviour needs to be rewarded with both financial and non-financial recognition. Generally, it is not the extent of the remuneration that matters but

the frequency. It is therefore advisable to offer rewards on every occasion when behaviour that is in line with the strategy is apparent. (Successful managers will actually create opportunities to give rewards of this kind.)

* The salary system should be *linked to the strategy*. If, for instance, Product Group A is to be stepped up and Product Group B maintained, the reward to the sales staff must be in line with this policy. The same considerations also apply to other fields of the company's activity.

* A *flexible use* of the salary systems. Many firms make the mistake of clinging for too long to a management system once it has been introduced (a salary system, for example). But management systems can become obsolescent, that is, they can become less attractive over time. They should therefore be re-examined at relatively short intervals (perhaps every two years) and if necessary redesigned.

Flexibility also means spontaneity. In one successful services firm with 'quality' as its SEP every departmental manager can give a member of his department a bonus of up to £100 on the spot if he does work of the appropriate quality. Since this is an extremely close interrelation between high performance and reward the system is very successful.

* *The principle of creativity*. Rewards will only be effective if they are not given schematically. For that reason creativity is needed to find new forms of recognition. If, for instance, the firm wants to build up 'innovation' as an SEP it could make the manager responsible for a new product a member of a special club once his turnover passes the one-million mark.

MANAGEMENT BY OBJECTIVES

It is generally recognized that staff need to have personal objectives, but in many companies the systems are too bureaucratic. Because an SEP shows the direction the company wants to move in it will enable the process of setting personal objectives to be simplified. Only a few (about 3) basic objectives should be set and these should be such as to make a strong contribution to developing the SEP.

PHYSICAL DISTRIBUTION SYSTEMS

Physical distribution systems must be aligned to new strategic objectives.

* Firstly, physical distribution systems must be such that products and markets with high priority can be dealt with first.

* Secondly, functional SEPs must also be taken into account. If, for instance, the company wants to build up a Strategic Excellence Position in customer service it must not allow a bad delivery service to result from too rigorous a policy on stockpiling.

PRODUCTION SYSTEMS

There is a particular danger of production systems being interpreted solely according to technical criteria. But production systems can differ widely within one industry, depending on the SEP the firm has chosen. Let us look at one example of this:

In the market for heating control systems an old-established company is concentrating on building up an SEP in productivity. It assembles long runs of standard models with a relatively high percentage of components produced in the firm. A recently established competitor is attacking it with 'tailor-made customer systems' as its SEP. Its production is flexible, with a relatively small amount produced in the firm. The higher unit costs this entails are counter-balanced by the better adjustment to customer requirements.

Similar principles apply to other management systems, such as finance and accounting, training and so on. The main principle is that these systems should first and foremost be structured according to the requirements of the SEP and not according to the traditions and habits of particular divisions or technical areas. Because this principle is often overlooked there are real chances to differentiate the firm from its competitors here: focusing all the management systems on the SEP will release a strong dynamic and so a genuine strategic impetus, and this will make the firm superior to its competitors.

The measures needed to adjust the management systems can again be worked out and written down in the form of action plans.

Organization

A newly developed strategy can deviate so much from the direction the company has been moving in so far that a reorganization is necessary. In that case a project is needed to develop and introduce a new structure that is better suited to the SEP and the grand strategy. However, complete reorganization is not often necessary and will not be discussed in any further detail here. It may be possible to take an evolutionary path and adjust the organization step by step to new conditions. The following principles are of particular importance in the concept of SEPs.

THE LOOSE–TIGHT CONCEPT
The concept which Peters and Waterman outline in their book, *In Search of Excellence* (1982), shows that in some areas a very tightly organized

and strictly controlled management is needed while in others direction can be looser, with more decentralization and delegation. The stricter management is obviously appropriate in the areas that are of fundamental importance for the company, in other words, for its Strategic Excellence Positions. In all the other areas more delegation will be possible.

FLEXIBILITY

In order to develop market-related Strategic Excellence Positions a company must always be aware of new developments and changes in customer requirements. Innovations need to be realized quickly and that is only possible with flexible forms of organization, such as task forces and, where necessary, co-operation agreements with external units and so on. Flexibility will only be achieved if bureaucratic instruments, such as job descriptions, are reduced.

Information systems

The strategic concept outlined here enables environmental opportunities to be exploited by defining and developing Strategic Excellence Positions.

It is extremely important to ensure that the development of the SEP is dynamic. Considerable mistakes can be made if this is overlooked, so if the strategy is to be successfully implemented the progress that is being made towards the SEP must be strictly monitored.

That in turn is only possible if clear and concrete information on the progress being made is available. The information systems in the company (reporting, statistics and accounting) need to be adjusted to these requirements, and action programmes should be developed to achieve this.

Management methods

There are two aspects that need to be considered here: the use of decision methods and the conduct of meetings.

DECISION METHODS

In the 1970s several business schools and institutions developed decision-making methods and trained managers in their use. The best known is probably the Kepner/Tregoe method (Kepner and Tregoe, 1965).

These methods can make a significant contribution to objective decision-making. The danger is that they may be used in isolation and handled technocratically. Too little consideration is then given to strategic viewpoints and the strategy loses impetus.

It is essential for management to take the basic strategy and especially the SEP into account in its daily decision-making. This can be done, for instance, by using the SEP as a criterion in evaluating alternatives.

CONDUCT OF MEETINGS

In many companies meetings are conducted following rules that have developed over time and are the result of the corporate culture. Attention also often focuses on quantitative aspects such as meeting budget requirements, achieving turnover goals, investment and so on.

But a strategy can only be properly implemented if the strategically relevant questions form the centre of attention. The management should therefore arrange the agenda in accordance with the strategic priorities. The SEP must be the main subject of the meeting!

Indirect means of strategy implementation

By using the direct means, instruments and methods available in the company the management can achieve a considerable degree of force in implementing its strategy. But more recent research has shown that this is far from enough. The direct means need to be supported by indirect measures.

The indirect means are more qualitative than the direct means. They are mainly designed to motivate the staff and ensure that their general attitude will further the implementation of the strategy.

Information

One of the most important indirect means of strategy implementation is to inform the staff about the new strategy. It is an indirect means because the staff are not given straight instructions but only a general account of the future direction the company is to take.

The staff need to know what the strategy is so that they can act accordingly in their day-to-day work. It is particularly important for them to adjust to the Strategic Excellence Position. If, for instance, the company has decided to make 'customer service' its SEP, the decision should constitute a challenge to all the members of the workforce to be particularly helpful to customers. The switchboard operator should make every effort to answer calls quickly and be friendly to callers. Drivers should be as helpful as possible to customers when delivering goods. The strategy is not simply a matter for the top management, it must be reflected in the behaviour of the staff right down to the smallest detail.

How can the staff be given the requisite information? The first possibility is to use the existing lines of command and communication. But then there is great danger that different people will receive different versions of the information. So it is better to call a meeting of the entire staff and give them the information in a carefully prepared form. Of course, this is only possible up to a certain size of firm and other ways have to be sought in larger firms. One is for the managing director to make a videotape outlining the new strategy and send copies to each department. But it is not enough simply to play the tape to the staff, they must be given an opportunity to discuss the new strategy and work out what the consequences are going to be for the work they have to do each day.

The oral information naturally has to be supplemented with written documentation on the grand strategy, and this can take the form of a text containing the main points together with the appropriate explanations.

This brings us to the problem of confidentiality. Information that is released to so many people will naturally become available to competitors. That makes it easier for them to develop counter-strategies and the management has to ask itself which is more important, informing the staff or keeping the strategy secret. The answer is self-evident. The staff will only be able to play their part in implementing the strategy if they know what it is. If the strategy is to be properly implemented, therefore, the information must necessarily be given openly and generally. Strategy papers that are kept locked up in the top management's safe are not likely to be very effective.

Of course there may be special situations – an oligopolist market structure, for instance – where it is necessary to restrict information and keep aspects of the strategy confidential. In that case the information should be limited to those points that are of particular importance for the staff. The written document that is to be distributed to the staff in the form of a guide sheet can also be kept in rather more general terms (Figure 5.5).

Experience shows that it is never enough to inform the staff only once. On the contrary, the management needs to take every opportunity to impress the workforce with the importance of the new direction.

The following are some of the measures that can be used for this:

ADJUSTMENT OF THE CORPORATE IDENTITY
The corporate identity conditions the whole picture presented by the company. If it conflicts with the chosen grand strategy, the strategy is unlikely to be generally accepted. The first task is therefore to re-examine the existing corporate identity in the light of the new SEP. That is a very difficult task and few public relations or advertising experts are trained to adjust a corporate identity to a new strategy. They generally focus on the industry or sector concerned or the technology used by the firm. A well-known advertising agency developed a corporate identity for a firm of architects which made it evident at a glance that this was a firm of planners and architects. But it took no account of the SEP the firm wanted to use, 'quality'. Although the manager responsible kept stressing that he wanted a corporate identity that took account of the concept of quality the agency were not able to provide this. The company had to go to

Fig 5.5 Corporate philosophy: the Hilti Company informs its staff about its strategy through a company guide sheet. This is a general version of the grand strategy.

1

In fastening technology we cover the requirements of the building and construction trades and of industry in general for tools and fasteners as well as providing the necessary advisory services. The activities start with the assessment of the demand and end with the satisfaction of the requirements.

2

As market performance we provide efficient, technically advanced, easily applicable and safe products and systems of optimum quality at appropriate price levels.

3

We consider the possession of adequate market shares to be a prime factor to safeguard the existence of the company. We obtain and protect our market shares by a policy of aggressive marketing for maximum economical market penetration.

4

Our operations are worldwide. As a multi-national corporation we recognize the necessity to expand and continuously develop our potential in marketing, production, research and development, finance, management and organization.

5

In all our business activities we try to maintain a fair and well balanced approach for sound, long-term relationships.

6

We aim for good co-operation with public authorities and other institutions.

7

In all our activities we try to maintain and improve environmental conditions.

8

Within the scope of our abilities we promote the personal and professional development of our employees and maintain a motivating working climate by actively involving our employees in company affairs.

9

We expect our employees to have high professional and personal qualifications and show the corresponding performance. We are prepared to remunerate our employees in accordance with the high standards of qualification and performance expected and will protect their welfare with adequate social benefit schemes.

10

We realize that the success of the company is decisively governed by our management and the required specialists. For this reason, we demand their full identification with the policies and goals of the corporation, a positive innovative attitude, flexibility and exemplary co-operative and cost-conscious behaviour.

11

We have to earn profits to safeguard the existence and long-term development of the company and provide a reasonable return on the capital invested.

12

Company affairs are always executed under the prime aspect of maintaining our sovereignty. i.e. the freedom to make our own decisions.

a different agency, and only after several attempts was a satisfactory solution found.

Since the concept of the corporate identity is all-embracing, all the means of communication available in the firm can come into play:

* stationery

* product description

* buildings

* office premises

* vehicle livery

* annual report

* the company periodical

* the customer news-sheet

* PR work

* advertising

* packaging

* and so on.

The extent to which the corporate identity should be aligned with the SEP cannot be stressed enough. Only when the staff are constantly reminded of the Strategic Exellence Position through the corporate identity in their daily work can they be expected to identify themselves with it in all the various jobs they have to do. If the SEP conflicts with the corporate identity on some points this will necessarily lead to friction; the implementation of the strategy will suffer and the strategic drive will slacken.

ARTICLES IN THE COMPANY PERIODICAL

The company's own publications for employees must be adjusted to the SEP and the management must take every opportunity to remind the staff of the strategic direction of the firm through editorials, articles and so on. Achievements by individual employees that have made a particular contribution to the strategy can be given special prominence.

ANNUAL REPORT

A company's annual report is primarily a means of giving information on the company's financial position, but it also offers a great opportunity to outline the strategy and stress the approach to implementing that strategy.

Besides the three possibilities outlined here there are a wide range of other means of achieving creative communication on a strategy that has been chosen. In the extremely successful company Wal-Mart, every employee wears a badge bearing the firm's motto: 'My job is to save you time and money.'

Only a constant and very full flow of information to the staff on the Strategic Excellence Positions and the company's general strategic direction will ensure that the strategy becomes a live experience and an integral part of their work. This in turn will generate more motivation and identification, and these are two of the main elements in successful company management.

The value of repetition cannot be overemphasized. SEPs can only be successfully developed if management keeps stressing the strategic goals, not only in written communications, with great insistence over an extended period of time. Oral communication is very important here and seminars, training sessions, workshops and press conferences are only some of the opportunities that can be used to press home the importance of the SEP.

Training

The management and staff of a company must think strategically. They must arrange their daily work to co-ordinate with the strategic priorities of the firm. That is the only way to realize the strategy.

Setting the right priorities is an extremely difficult task. The management will only succeed in it if they conceive of the strategy as a whole and are able to derive concrete guidelines for their own action from it.

This is a process of learning that can best be done in workshops, each of which should be attended by between 15 and 20 of the management staff.

The workshop should start with the grand strategy, with which all the managers should be familiar. So far this has been worked out for the company as a whole (or maybe individual divisions or product areas), and the purpose of the workshop is to produce specific action plans for each participant's area.

The first step is therefore for the managers to find *core capabilities* that are related to their departments. These are the equivalent of the Strategic Excellence Positions formulated at company level. They are qualities in a department that will be effective over the longer term and will enable the staff to do their work with above-average success.

The core capabilities can be identified on the basis of:

* the Strategic Excellence Positions defined for the company

* the present situation in the department concerned (the available strengths and weaknesses)

* the environment of the department and the opportunities that can be derived from this.

So each manager (or departmental head) establishes the core capabilities for his area by a brief survey of the current situation.

The main emphasis must be on ensuring the maximum degree of correspondence between the core capabilities and the firm's SEP. That will make an essential contribution to developing the strategic thrust of the firm.

The departmental managers can then draw up action plans directed to developing the core capabilities. Once this work has been done there will be clearly defined Strategic Excellence Positions for the firm as a whole (or each division, etc.) and core capabilities for the individual departments. The firm's SEPs show the areas the top management should concentrate on. The core capabilities show where the emphasis must lie at department level.

A manager in a firm with 'quality' as its SEP will have to concentrate mainly on questions of quality in his personal style and approach to work. The finance manager – again assuming that the firm's SEP is 'quality' – may perhaps see the core capabilities for his department as immediate and accurate invoicing, day-to-day reminders and immediate response to customer queries.

A feature of the SEP concept is that the SEP laid down in the grand strategy is not an abstraction applicable to the company as a whole but a personal matter for each individual employee. It should become a guideline for the behaviour of each individual member of the management.

Every firm has other important members of staff beside the management as a whole and the departmental heads. There are the foremen, members of staff departments and highly qualified skilled workers. To ensure that the strategy becomes a *living experience* on the broadest possible basis these people also need to spotlight their personal core capabilities. This process is analogous to that for individual departments. In the end result each of these employees should have a set of personal core capabilities.

The concept outlined here makes it possible to link the daily work of each member of the management directly with the strategy. Moreover, the personal core capabilities identified on the basis of the strategy should largely coincide with personal annual objectives. Accordingly, the process of management can be simplified and bound up more closely with the strategy objectives.

Experience has shown that as a rule a two-day workshop is enough to work out the departmental and personal core capabilities and plan the actions that are needed to develop them and implement the strategy. These workshops can be conducted by someone on the company staff or an outside consultant. Attention should never focus exclusively on the factual identification of the core capabilities: the meetings should also serve as an occasion to increase the participants' motivation and gain support for the new strategy. The spirit that can be created can go a long way to help the strategy to a breakthrough even under difficult environmental conditions.

Work on the strategy in meetings of this nature will only take up a small amount of the time that a company generally allocates to training. The management development or training department will be organizing a large number of other seminars and specialized training courses as well. In many companies the effectiveness of these can be greatly increased if the general concept is improved. Many of these seminars and courses are taken by specialists who may be excellently qualified in their particular field but who are not really practised in integrating strategic considerations into their training measures. Sales training courses, for instance, are generally directed by a sales specialist who sees the whole complex of selling and its problems exclusively in terms of his specialized knowledge. But in the strategic view, sales training in a company with 'image-building' as an SEP is quite different from sales training in a firm with 'market shares' as an SEP. In the first case selling is more of a representational task, since the sales staff should maintain good relations with their customers and offer an excellent service, while in the other, where the company is aiming to gain market shares, the emphasis should be on training high-performance sellers. Selling is not necessarily the same if the SEP differs. It would therefore be wrong to train the staff to use the same method regardless of the overall aim of the company (though this is often the case). The same, of course, applies to other training measures, such as leadership training, project management training and EDP courses. More attention should be given to this principle when teaching the specialized knowledge required in a particular industry or sector. A course for bank cashiers, for example, should differ according to whether the bank has 'quality' as its SEP or 'a broad range of services'.

If a company really wants to develop a massive strategic thrust, the SEP must become the main focal point of the training.

In a company with 'quality' and 'innovation' as SEPs a seminar on computers should deal with quality promotion and innovation as well as questions concerning EDP. The subjects should always be seen in terms of the appropriate SEP. That is the only way to make sure that the SEP becomes the focus of the employees' thinking and action. Long and wearisome explanations on the strategy will then be superfluous. That will also enable the SEP to exercise a lasting influence on the corporate culture.

It is important to recognize that staff development is a crucial factor in the SEP concept. The SEP is closely bound up with the capabilities available in the firm and training is a central instrument for developing those capabilities.

Corporate culture

In Chapter 4 we saw how the corporate culture is subjected to detailed consideration during the process of information analysis in order to provide a clear 'corporate profile'.

We have also seen (Law 10 on the management of SEPs) that a new company strategy can only be developed successfully if it accords with the corporate culture. If that is not the case then

* either a strategy must be chosen that does accord with the corporate culture,

* or the corporate culture will have to be adapted.

It is a question of central concern how the management is to create a culture that is oriented to the company's grand strategy and primary SEP, i.e. how to adapt the existing culture and bring it more into line with the strategy that has been chosen (Figure 5.6).

The corporate culture is the complex of opinions, norms and values that determine the behaviour of the management and staff. It is not easy to influence

Fig 5.6 Appropriate measures are needed to adjust the corporate culture to the strategy.

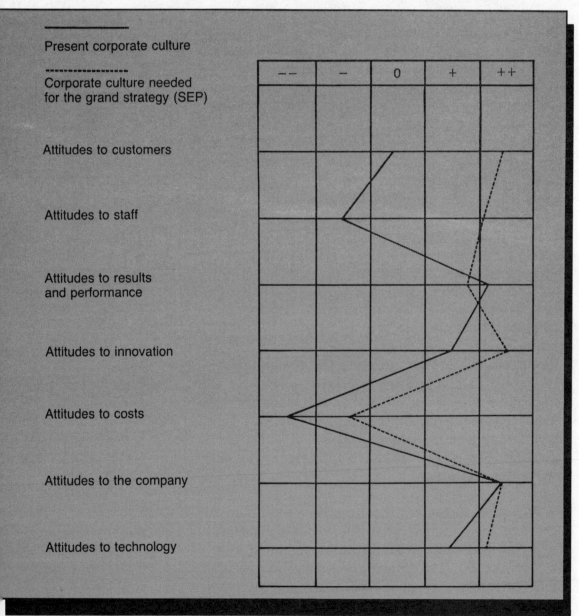

these opinions, norms and values. The management has to choose a procedure that will suit the specific situation of the firm, but it is nevertheless possible to offer a few general guidelines.

Measures that are to affect a corporate culture should create strong opinions, norms and values in the areas that are important for the SEP that has been chosen. If the primary SEP is 'distribution service' the management must take steps to ensure that all the members of the firm attach the very greatest importance to friendly relations with customers and a rapid and smooth supply of goods. One element in the culture, for instance, could be the principle that orders must be carried out on the same day, that the drivers – no matter what the cost – must see that the customer gets the goods the day they are ordered and ensure that everything goes smoothly for the customer. In a steel company instructions were given to the drivers to take the steel direct to the place where it was to be used, unload it and store it under cover, and this brought considerable competitive advantages.

In principle, any measure that is taken to implement the strategy will affect the cultural values and norms in the company. If the management, for instance, sets certain signals through consistent and skilful action plans this will have an influence on the staff's opinions and values. This is even clearer in the management systems: a good salary system, which gives rewards for strategic behaviour, will have a strong impact on the corporate culture.

The direct measures that are taken to implement the strategy will have an influence on the corporate culture which should not be underestimated. But the management will need to support these direct measures with a number of carefully chosen indirect measures. Why are these so important?

We know from anthropologists that non-verbal communication is very much older than logical, rational communication. Precisely because non-verbal communication is so primeval it has a very much stronger influence on our behaviour than verbal, logical or rational communication. The following example will illustrate this: a company chief who has so far been very cost-oriented announces that he intends to develop 'innovation' as an SEP. But at meetings and so on his gestures, facial expression and posture (i.e. his non-verbal communication) make it plain to his staff that he is much less concerned with innovation than with costs. The staff register this non-verbal communication immediately and however much the boss may proclaim his intention, orally or in written memoranda, of developing 'innovation' as an SEP no one believes him.

So the indirect measures used to develop the corporate culture must communicate the essence of the strategy non-verbally. They must be addressed mainly to the emotions of the recipients, and if they are successful the response should be behaviour that is in line with the strategy. What indirect measures can the management use?

SYMBOLIC ACTS

Symbolic acts can be the central element in creating a corporate culture. They are non-verbal acts designed to stress the high value the management attaches to certain behaviour or a certain matter. One example will serve:

The head of NCR, John Patterson, once had the desk of a manager who had failed to meet his sales targets brought out in front of the building and set on fire before the astonished sales managers. He pointed to the burning desk and roared: 'You're fired!' News of this symbolic act went round NCR like a fire itself. Patterson had found a very dramatic way of showing that any manager who failed to meet his targets could not be sure of his job. The symbolic action was very much more effective than a memo on the same subject would have been.

Symbolic acts by the top management need a certain amount of drama and intensity. What matters in implementing the strategy is to find symbolic acts that will illustrate the behaviour needed and held to be particularly desirable and valuable. It is worth holding brief brainstorming sessions to create ideas for symbolic acts that can be used to support the implementation of strategy.

CEREMONIES

Ceremonies on firms' anniversaries, year-end meetings, meetings to mark promotion and so on are naturally of a symbolic nature. When forward strategies are being implemented it is therefore extremely important to utilize the opportunities they present to underline the strategy. The ceremonies at Mary Kay Cosmetics, for instance, are famous. Every year a meeting is held at which employees who have made a particular contribution to implementing the strategy are given special recognition. The highlight of the meeting is the moment when a pink Cadillac is presented to the most successful woman customer consultant. This makes it evident to all the firm that 'customer consultancy' is of primary importance as an SEP. It is also a most impressive example of non-verbal communication. Other companies, of course, may have very different, but equally effective, ceremonies.

STORIES AND ANECDOTES

For thousands of years story-telling has been a part of human culture. We all know of the story-tellers who entertained people at fairs and bazaars with fairy stories and other tales. This kind of story-telling always has a moral – some behaviour is shown to be desirable in its particular culture, while other behaviour is condemned and punished. Our historical evolution has enabled us to see the point of these stories and we accept the values they convey. Indeed, most people learn much more easily and more effectively through stories of this kind and examples than from abstractions or logical argument.

Use can be made of the possibilities for learning of this kind in creating corporate culture. Let us take one example: a very successful entrepreneur, who founded his business at the beginning of the 1950s and now employs several thousand people, takes every opportunity to tell his staff stories from the early days of the firm. One is that during a difficult period he heard that one of his customers was about to give a very large order. He went to the customer straight away and then spent the night working out his offer. He took it to the customer himself at eight o'clock the following morning. The man was so impressed that he gave him the order. This story is an excellent example of how important personal engagement is in selling; but it also symbolizes the importance of the business approach in everything we do.

WORKSHOPS

The ways of influencing the corporate culture outlined so far are mainly informal. But of course action plans and lists of ideas can be developed for this purpose as well. Beside the rather informal measures there is also the possibility of deliberately and directly creating a corporate culture. Again this can be done through workshops. The first step is to draw up a profile of the current corporate culture and discuss it. Then groups should be formed to discuss what kind of culture would best suit the new strategy. Lists of the new values and norms should be drawn up, since these will determine the future corporate culture. Here too the participants can decide on concrete actions that can be used to get the new culture going.

The problem in creating a corporate culture will often be not so much a lack of the necessary techniques as that the behaviour of the management has developed over many years and become a firmly programmed tradition. It is not rationally directed but unconscious. That is why the new corporate culture cannot simply be rationally promoted and developed and a long and difficult process of reorientation may be needed.

Management appointment/promotion

The way managers are deployed can be very important in the implementation of strategies.

The first requirement is to use the ablest members of the management where a strategic breakthrough is needed. In the SEP concept this means that the ablest members of the management should be employed on developing the primary SEP. Promotion is of course closely linked with management deployment, and promotion should first go to those whose personality and occupational training and experience make them especially fit to develop the Strategic Excellence Position. Here too it is evident that a measure of this kind will not only directly further the implementation of the strategy; it may well have a symbolic character which will set signals. An excellent example of this is the change in the direction of General Electric. After the company had been headed for many years by finance specialists the Board signalled its reorientation towards technology and innovation by appointing the head of research, John Welch, as its new chairman in 1981.

Conclusion

This book has presented a simple and consistent concept – the concept of the Strategic Exellence Position – which allows a company to concentrate on the factors that are most important for success. The book has introduced the ideas of SEP management in four main stages:

STAGE 1

Stage 1 (Chapters 1, 2 and 3) introduced the principles of corporate strategy and the ten laws of SEP management.

Strategic superiority can be achieved in three ways:

* differentiation

* low costs

* good timing

Strategic Excellence Positions are derived from the principles of corporate strategy and thus link strategic principles and strategy development.

STAGE 2

Stage 2 (first half of Chapter 4) was a discussion of information analysis as a basis for the development of a grand strategy.

An information analysis must take into consideration:

* qualitative data

* quantitative data

* timeframe of future developments

STAGE 3

Stage 3 (second half of Chapter 4) showed how to formulate a grand strategy. A grand strategy defines the future direction of the company. The cornerstones of the grand strategy are the Strategic Excellence Positions to be developed.

STAGE 4

Stage 4 (Chapter 5) showed how to implement a grand strategy. Implementation can be successful only if all management efforts support it.

The complete process is summarized opposite.

The SEP concept is based on a philosophy which can be outlined as follows:

1. A company cannot survive in the long term without a clear direction. If companies stop looking to the future they degenerate rapidly into bureaucratic administrations. When they lose their innovative force they also lose the motive to survive. Therefore, a successful strategy must look to the future and must be based on growth through innovation and change.

The SEP concept includes the idea of building for the future. A company aiming to develop a Strategic Excellence Position needs to be forward-looking and it must adopt a constructive approach.

2. The whole strategic concept outlined here is

The system of strategic management: a survey.

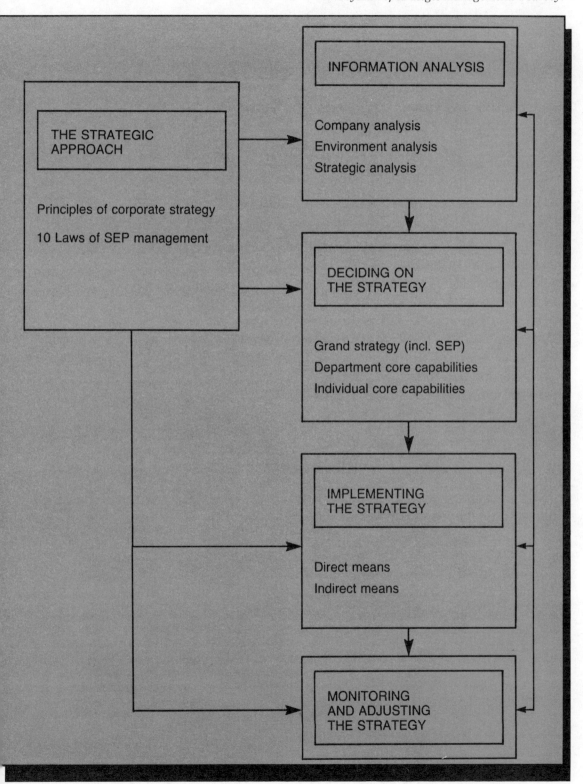

designed to enable the company to recognize opportunities in its environment and utilize its own strengths. Plans based on defensive strategies have been deliberately ignored: I regard it as wrong in principle for companies to try to defend a position through cartels or restrictive practices. History clearly shows that bastions of this kind cannot be held. That applies in the military sphere as well, as shown by the Maginot line, the Great Wall of China, the Limes and so on. Only flexibility in attack will lead to success.

3. A company can survive over the longer term only if it makes a profit. For that reason the company's success plays a crucial role in the concept as a whole. Success is never due to a chance coincidence of factors; a company can succeed only if it develops strong and genuine capabilities. A company will be profitable if it offers particular goods or services that are needed in its environment. That is also the basis for a healthy profit trend over the longer term.

4. A further central element is motivation and the *unité de doctrine* that this entails. Only motivated and enthusiastic employees will over the longer term be able to meet the high requirements of SEP management. The necessary motivation can be achieved in different ways:

   * Simply defining a clear direction for the company in the form of a grand strategy and especially an SEP will increase motivation. The employees will realize that there is a clear direction and they will know where they are heading.

   * A forward-looking approach will also increase motivation. It will make attitudes such as holding on to or defending a position or looking for redundancies superfluous. It becomes the

declared aim of the management to lead the company into a prosperous future.

* Deciding on Strategic Excellence Positions harmonizes the entire action in a company. Threatened conflicts between departments and interest groups can more easily be avoided. The forces are not fragmented in internal strife.

* Implementing the strategy requires dynamic action. The early results achieved by this will in turn increase motivation.

* Ultimately, the whole process of strategic management is a matter for a team. The main tasks are tackled in workshops which all the senior managers should attend. Planning is not carried out by a highly sophisticated staff department but by the line management. When the strategy is being implanted the strategic idea should be implanted down to the lowest levels of management. The middle and lower management should also have the opportunity to go through the strategic thought process and make their contribution to the strategy. Training in implementing the strategy will also increase motivation.

    All the activities to increase motivation should add up to the strategic thrust that is so important. It will be this strategic drive that decides whether a company can cope with the future successfully or not.

5. If we succeed in reducing the defensive attitude that is now so widespread through a future-oriented strategy and by breathing a new spirit into company management, entrepreneurs will be able to exercise the great political responsibility they bear to their environment. Not only will existing jobs be safer and new jobs created; even more important is the positive spirit that can be

transferred from the company to the community as a whole. The resultant belief in the future will help us to solve the very considerable problems we face in the world today.

Bibliography

Abell, D. F. and Hammond, J. S., *Strategic Market Planning*, New Jersey 1979.

Abernathy, W. J. and Wayne, K., 'Limits of the Learning Curve', *Harvard Business Review*, Sept.-Oct. 1974.

Ansoff, H. I., *Strategic Management*, The Macmillan Press, London 1979.

Argenti, J., *Corporate Collapse. The Causes and Symptoms*, McGraw-Hill, London 1976.

Ball, R., 'At BMW, Performance Counts', *Fortune*, 30 June 1980.

Bennis, W. and Nanus, B., *Leaders. The Strategies For Taking Charge*, Harper & Row, New York 1985.

Buzzel, R. D., 'Product Quality', *PIMS Letter on Business Strategy, Nr. 4,* The Strategic Planning Institute, Cambridge, Mass. 1978.

Clausewitz, C. von, *Vom Kriege,* 19th ed., Dümmlers Verlag, Bonn 1980. English translations: *On War,* ed. and transl. M. Howard and P. Paret (Princeton NJ, Princeton University Press, 1976); *On War* (abridged), transl. J. J. Graham, ed. A. Rapoport (Harmondsworth, Penguin, 1982).

Deal, T. E. and Kennedy, A. A., *Corporate Cultures,* Addison-Wesley, Reading, Mass. 1982.

De Lorean, J. Z., *On a Clear Day You Can See General Motors,* New York 1980.

Deming, W. E., 'What Top Management Must Do', *Business Week,* 20 July 1981.

Drucker, P. F., *Management,* Heinemann, London 1974.

Gray, C. S., 'Total Quality Control in Japan, Less Inspection, Lower Cost', *Business Week,* 20 July 1981.

Hall, W. K., 'Survival strategies in a hostile environment', *Harvard Business Review,* Sept.-Oct. 1980.

Henderson, B. D., *Perspectives on Experience,* 4th ed., Herder & Herder, Frankfurt/New York 1974.

Kepner, C. H. and Tregoe, B. B., *The Rational Manager,* McGraw-Hill, New York 1965.

Kotler, P., *Marketing Management,* 5th ed., Prentice-Hall, Englewood Cliffs 1984.

Levitt, T., 'Marketing success through differentiation of anything', *Harvard Business Review,* Jan.-Feb. 1980.

Levitt, T., *The Marketing Imagination,* The Free Press, New York 1983.

Liddell Hart, B. H., *Strategy,* 4th ed., New American Library, New York 1974; Faber & Faber, London 1967.

Ogger, G., *Kauf Dir einen Kaiser,* Zurich 1979.

Ohmae, K., *The Mind of the Strategist,* McGraw-Hill, New York 1982; Penguin, Harmondsworth 1983.

Peters, T. J., 'Putting Excellence into Management', *Business Week,* 21 July 1980.

Peters, T. J. and Waterman, R. H., *In Search of Excellence – Lessons from America's Best-Run Companies*, Harper & Row, New York 1982.

Petre, P. D., 'Meet the lean, mean new IBM', *Fortune*, 13 June 1983, pp. 68 et seq.

Porter, M. E., *Competitive Strategy*, The Free Press, New York 1980.

Pümpin, C., *Management strategischer Erfolgspositionen. Das SEP-Konzept als Grundlage wirkungsvoller Unternehmungsführung*, 3rd ed., Haupt, Berne/Stuttgart 1986.

Pümpin, C., 'Unternehmenskultur, Unternehmensstrategie und Unternehmenserfolg', *gdi-impuls 2/84*, Rüschlikon 1984.

Schoeffler, S., Buzzell, R. D. and Heanay, D. F., 'Impact of Strategic Planning on Profit Performance', *Harvard Business Review*, March-April 1974.

Schoeffler, S., 'Capital-Intensive Technology vs ROI: A Strategic Assessment', *Management Review*, Sept. 1978.

Sloan, A. P., *My Years with General Motors*, New York 1964.

Index